*Great Careers*

# Communications, the Arts, and Computers

*with a High School Diploma*

# Titles in the *Great Careers* series

# Great Careers

# Communications, the Arts, and Computers

## with a High School Diploma

### Kenneth C. Mondschein

Ferguson Publishing
*An imprint of Infobase Publishing*

*Great Careers with a High School Diploma*
## Communications, the Arts, and Computers

Ferguson
An imprint of Infobase Publishing
132 West 31st Street
New York, NY 10001

ISBN-13:978-0-8160-7044-2

Library of Congress Cataloging-in-Publication Data

Great careers with a high school diploma. — 1st ed.
     v. cm.
  Includes bibliographical references and index
  Contents: [1] Food, agriculture, and natural resources — [2] Construction and trades — [3] Communications, the arts, and computers — [4] Sales, marketing, business, and finance — [5] Personal care services, fitness, and education — [6] Health care, medicine, and science — [7] Hospitality, human services, and tourism — [8] Public safety, law, and security — [9] Manufacturing and transportation — [10] Armed forces.
   ISBN-13: 978-0-8160-7046-6 (v.1)
   ISBN-10: 0-8160-7046-6 (v.1)
   ISBN-13: 978-0-8160-7043-5 (v.2)
   ISBN-10: 0-8160-7043-1 (v.2)
  [etc.]
  1. Vocational guidence — United Sates. 2. Occupations — United Sates. 3. High school graduates — Employment — United Sates.
   HF5382.5.U5G677 2007
   331.702'330973 — dc22

                                                                2007029883

Produced by Print Matters, Inc.
Text design by A Good Thing, Inc.
Cover design by Salvatore Luongo

Printed in the United States of America

Sheridan PMI 10 9 8 7 6 5 4 3 2

This book is printed on acid-free paper.

# Contents

# How to Use This Book

This book, part of the Great Careers with a High School Diploma series, highlights in-demand careers that require no more than a high school diploma or the general educational development (GED) credential and offer opportunities for personal growth and professional advancement to motivated readers who are looking for a field that's right for them. The focus throughout is on the fastest-growing jobs with the best potential for advancement in the field. Readers learn about future prospects while discovering jobs they may never have heard of.

Knowledge—of yourself and about a potential career—is a powerful tool in launching yourself professionally. This book tells you how to use it to your advantage, explore job opportunities, and identify a good fit for yourself in the working world.

Each chapter provides the essential information needed to find not just a job but a career that draws on your particular skills and interests. All chapters include the following features:

- ✴ "Is This Job for You?" presents a set of questions for you to answer about yourself to help you learn if you have what it takes to work in a given career.
- ✴ "Let's Talk Money" and "Lets Talk Trends" provide at a glance crucial information about salary ranges and employment prospects.
- ✴ "What You'll Do" provides descriptions of the essentials of each job.
- ✴ "Where You'll Work" relates the details of the settings and the rules and patterns typical of that field.
- ✴ "Your Typical Day" provides details about what a day on the job involves for each occupation.
- ✴ "The Inside Scoop" presents firsthand information from someone working in the field.
- ✴ "What You Can Do Now" provides advice on getting prepared for your future career.
- ✴ "What Training You'll Need" discusses state requirements, certifications, and courses or other training you may need as you get started on your new career path.
- ✴ "How to Talk Like a Pro" defines a few key terms that give a feel for the occupation.

✴ "How to Find a Job" gives the practical how-tos of landing a position.

✴ "Secrets for Success" and "Reality Check" share inside information on getting ahead.

✴ "Some Other Jobs to Think About" lists similar related careers to consider.

✴ "How You Can Move Up" outlines how people in each occupation turn a job into a career, advancing in responsibility and earnings power.

✴ "Web Sites to Surf" lists Web addresses of trade organizations and other resources providing more information about the career.

In addition to a handy comprehensive index, the back of the book features an appendix providing invaluable information on job hunting strategies and techniques. This section provides general tips on interviewing, constructing a strong résumé, and gathering professional references. Use this book to discover a career that seems right for you—the tools to get you where you want to be are at your fingertips.

# Introduction

For millions of Americans, life after high school means stepping into the real world. Each year more than 900,000 of the nation's 2.8 million high school graduates go directly into the workforce. Clearly, college isn't for everyone. Many people learn best by using their hands rather than by sitting in a classroom. Others find that the escalating cost of college puts it beyond reach, at least for the time being. During the 2005–2006 school year, for instance, tuition and fees at a four-year public college averaged $5,491, not including housing costs, according to The College Board.

The good news is that there's a wide range of exciting, satisfying careers available without a four-year bachelor's degree or even a two-year associate's degree. Great Careers with a High School Diploma highlights specific, in-demand careers in which individuals who have only a high school diploma or the general educational development (GED) credential can find work, with or without further training (outside of college). These jobs span the range from apprentice electronics technician to chef, teacher's assistant, Webpage designer, sales associate, and lab technician. The additional training that some of these positions require may be completed either on the job, through a certificate program, or during an apprenticeship that combines entry-level work and class time.

Happily, there's plenty of growth in the number of jobs that don't require a college diploma. That growth is fastest for positions that call for additional technical training or a certificate of proficiency. The chief economist at the Economic Policy Foundation, a think tank specializing in employment issues, notes that there are simply more of these positions available than there are workers to fill them. In fact, only 23 percent of the jobs available in the coming years will require a four-year degree or higher, the foundation reports.

It's often said that higher education is linked to higher earnings. But this is not the whole story. Correctional officer, computer network technician, and electrician are just a few of the careers that offer strong income-earning potential. What's more, the gap that exists between the wages of high school graduates and those with college degrees has begun to close slightly. Between 2000 and 2004, the yearly earnings of college graduates dropped by 5.6 percent while the earnings of high school graduates increased modestly by 1.6 percent according to the Economic Policy Foundation. High school graduates earn a median yearly income of $26,104, according the U.S. Census Bureau.

So what career should a high school graduate consider? The range is so broad that Great Careers with a High School Diploma includes 10 volumes, each based on related career fields from the Department of Labor's career clusters. Within each volume approximately 10 careers are profiled, encouraging readers to focus on a wide selection of job possibilities, some of which readers may not even know exist. To enable readers to narrow their choices, each chapter offers a self-assessment quiz that helps answer the question, "Is this career for me?" What's more, each job profile includes an insightful look at what the position involves, highlights of a typical day, insight into the work environment, and an interview with someone on the job.

An essential part of the decision to enter a particular field includes how much additional training is needed. Great Careers features opportunities that require no further academic study or training beyond high school as well as those that do. Readers in high school can start prepping for careers immediately through volunteer work, internships, academic classes, technical programs, or career academies. (Currently, for instance, one in four students concentrates on a vocational or technical program.) For each profile, the best ways for high school students to prepare are featured in a "What You Can Do Now" section.

For readers who are called to serve in the armed forces, this decision also provides an opportunity to step into a range of careers. Every branch of the armed forces from the army to the coast guard offers training in areas including administrative, construction, electronics, health care, and protective services. One volume of Great Careers with a High School Diploma is devoted to careers than can be reached with military training. These range from personnel specialist to aircraft mechanic.

Beyond military options, other entry-level careers provide job seekers with an opportunity to test-drive a career without a huge commitment. Compare the ease of switching from being a bank teller to a sales representative, for instance, with that of investing three years and tens of thousands of dollars into a law school education, only to discover a dislike for the profession. Great Careers offers not only a look at related careers, but also ways to advance in the field. Another section, "How to Find a Job," provides job-hunting tips specific to each career. This includes, for instance, advice for teacher assistants to develop a portfolio of their work. As it turns out,

employers of entry-level workers aren't looking for degrees and academic achievements. They want employability skills: a sense of responsibility, a willingness to learn, discipline, flexibility, and above all, enthusiasm. Luckily, with 100 jobs profiled in Great Careers with a High School Diploma, finding the perfect one to get enthusiastic about is easier than ever.

*Meet interesting people*

# Grip, Stagehand, Set-Up Worker

*Help to make films, television shows, and dramatic productions*

*Work in an exciting industry*

# *Grip, Stagehand, Set-Up Worker*

When you watch a movie or TV show or go to a play or rock concert, all you usually see are the actors or musicians. Behind the scenes, dozens or even hundreds of people have worked hard to make what you see possible. Grips, stagehands, and set-up workers do everything needed in a stage or screen production, from placing the lights and holding sound booms on a TV show to changing the scenery in an opera or making sure that a sound stage set up to look like a diner has plates and napkins. Set and exhibit designers and those in related fields hold about 34,000 jobs in the music industry in the United States, and about 10,000 positions in the non-music arts and entertainment sector, according to the U.S. Bureau of Labor Statistics.

## *Is This Job for You?*

To find out if being a grip, stagehand, or set-up worker is right for you, read each of the following questions and answer "Yes" or "No."

Yes No **1.** Can you move to where a job is, if necessary?
Yes No **2.** Can you work long or irregular hours?
Yes No **3.** Do you take directions well?
Yes No **4.** Are you very organized?
Yes No **5.** Are you physically strong?
Yes No **6.** Do you have a good creative "eye?"
Yes No **7.** Do you work well under pressure?
Yes No **8.** Are you willing to start at the bottom?
Yes No **9.** Are you a team player?
Yes No **10.** Do you have good communications skills?

If you answered "Yes" to most of these questions, you might be right for a career as a grip, stagehand, or set-up worker. To find out more about these jobs, read on.

## *What You'll Do*

Grips, stagehands, and set-up workers do literally everything that is not acting, directing, production, making something, or another specialized skill such as using a camera.

## Let's Talk Trends

It is difficult to estimate growth in the number of grips, stagehands, and set-up workers. There may be less growth, due to many movies now being filmed overseas. Since everyone wants to be in show business, there will also be a lot of competition for jobs in this industry.

*Grips* work in movies. They cooperate closely with both the lighting and camera departments to make sure the cameras are in place and the lights are set up. On union jobs, grips do not touch the cameras or lights themselves, but they do everything else that will handle how the light diffuses across the set.

*Stagehands* work in theater. They may find themselves working in lights, sound, operating the *fly system* as part of the fly crew, or a number of other jobs.

*Set-up workers* may find themselves anywhere from marking the places where the actors will stand to rigging heavy lights hundreds of feet above the ground. In large production houses, responsibilities are carefully defined. For instance, suppose a scene calls for a swordfight to break out on the deck of a ship between two actors playing pirates. *Wardrobe* will handle the pirate costumes, *property* will handle the swords and everything an actor will touch, use, or carry, while a *set dresser* will set up all the background props, such as ropes, rigging, belaying pins, and cannonballs. The *swing gang* makes last-minute changes to the set before filming, such as moving a cannon that is interfering with the camera.

## Let's Talk Money

It is hard to estimate grips', stagehands', and set-up workers' earnings, because so much of the work is irregular and also because of the wide variety of positions. The median income for all workers in arts and entertainment is $313 per week. Workers with regular jobs, such as with opera companies and Hollywood studios, will tend to be paid according to their specialty, such as carpenters and electricians. Workers who are union members will be paid according to union rates. For instance, the Motion Picture Studio Grips' Union requires a minimum hourly wage of $28.30.

## *Who* You'll Work For

✴ TV production companies

✴ Movie studios

✴ Local TV stations

✴ Production companies

✴ Theaters and theater companies

✴ Musicians and touring companies

## *Where* You'll Work

Many openings for grips, stagehands, and set-up workers are in Los Angeles or New York, since these cities both have large theater scenes and because many movies, television shows, and commercials are shot there. Grips, stagehands, and set-up workers usually work in theaters, studios, and sound stages, but for filming on location, you may need to travel to distant parts of the country or the world. Some jobs are exclusively on the road. For instance, *roadies* go along with a touring production or band to do their set-up for them in various venues.

Hours in the entertainment industry can be very irregular, with 14- to 18-hour days one month followed by several weeks of unemployment. Because of this, it can be difficult to estimate what your earnings will be for a particular year. On the other hand, if you are working for certain productions, such as a Broadway show, you might have a fairly regular work schedule. The motion picture industry, in general, tends to provide more irregular work than is found with regular live productions.

Some of the work can be strenuous or dangerous, such as rigging lights high off the ground, but the danger you will be exposed to is usually limited by contract. Employers in the entertainment industry are required to take care of their employees' well-being.

## *Your* Typical Day

Here are the highlights of a typical day for a set-up worker.

✔ **Up at dawn.** Today you'll be working in the property department of the new pirate film *Swashbucklers of the Sargasso*. The call is for 6 a.m., which means that you're dressed and out of your hotel room before the sun is up.

# The Inside Scoop: Q&A

**Sandra Kay Muncie**
**Set-up worker**
**Los Angeles, California**

**Q:** *How did you get your job?*

**A:** I initially started working at Roger Corman doing Craft Service, meaning I bought all the snacks for the crew. It was the only job I could get that paid money that was actually in film production. The film industry is notorious for non-paying internships. I eventually landed in Property, which is basically anything the actor handles, your department is responsible for.

**Q:** *What do you like best about your job?*

**A:** I love the variety of people I have met in the film industry. Every type of person you could possibly imagine is in some way or another incorporated into the film industry on some level. It's a very dynamic community.

**Q:** *What's the most challenging part of your job?*

**A:** The most challenging part of my job is probably the schedule and the hours. I have worked both a lot of television and film, and it's not uncommon to work a 16-hour day. Once in a while is not that bad, but try doing it every day for a few weeks, and you know what true exhaustion is. I'm pregnant with my first child right now, and I'm trying to figure out how to juggle work and family life. My husband is a special effects engineer and cameraman, and he travels a lot. It's not unusual for him to be on location for six months at a time. I have stayed closer to home because I have worked more on television series the past four years.

**Q:** *What are the keys to success as a grip, stagehand, or set-up worker?*

**A:** Personally, I think everybody has their own path to success, and don't listen too much what other people tell you are the secrets. What works for one person isn't going to necessarily work for another. You do need to be dedicated to what you do, and that goes for anything. I don't think that's a secret. Plus, it's always easier to be dedicated to something that you love.

✔ **Set it up . . . and set it up again.** Your job doesn't end after you hand the actors their prop swords and set up the pirate ship to look like it's from the 1700s. The director wants take after take, and after each, you need to restack the cannonballs, make sure the rigging's tight, and everything's generally shipshape. In the meantime, you wait around for when you're needed.

✔ **Break it down.** The scene finally finishes shooting around 11 p.m., but your day's not over—you still have to put away all those cannonballs!

## What You Can Do Now

✦ Get to know people. The entertainment industry is a very social one, and contacts you make now can help you later on.

✦ Work in school productions and amateur theater. Do everything you can to gain experience.

✦ Study everything you can about how movies and TV shows are filmed.

## What Training You'll Need

Most grips, stagehands, and set-up workers are trained informally on the job. This is definitely an industry where you learn by doing and where experience counts. For this reason, it is best to get as much experience as possible. Try to join community theater or independent movie productions. There are also film schools that can teach you some of the basics of the motion picture industry. Such schools can be expensive, however, and completing a course is no guarantee of getting a job.

Another way to learn the basics is through an entry-level job, summer employment, or an internship. There you will learn to set up lights and scenery, handle equipment, make scene changes, and do everything else that a grip, stagehand, or set-up worker does.

## How to Talk Like a Pro

Here are a few words you'll hear as a grip, stagehand, or set-up worker:

✦ **Cutting light** To "cut" light is to focus, refract it, reflect it, or diffuse it so that a scene is lit exactly the way it should be.

✴ **Fly system** The system of weights and pulleys used to raise and lower scenery and other items in a theatrical production.

✴ **Prop** Short for "theatrical property"—the physical objects that actors interact with. Often humorously defined as anything that gets in your way during a scene change. This may include actors.

## *How* to Find a Job

In the entertainment industry everyone needs friends, and grips, stagehands, and set-up workers are no exceptions. Knowing people in the industry can help you find openings and, more importantly, get you hired. The best way to meet people, of course, is to work in the industry. This is why internships and volunteer experience can be so important—they show that you know what you're doing. To find a position, ask local production companies and theater groups if they need any workers.

You can often find paying jobs for grips, stagehands, and set-up workers advertised in newspapers, free weeklies, and trade publications. Look also on Web sites such as Craigslist (http://www.craigs list.org) or Variety.com.

While getting your foot in the door is important, it is your reputation that will get you more work. People in charge of productions want to know that they can count on you. Always be sure to do a good job, and you can count on recommendations and references later on.

## *Secrets* for Success

See the suggestions below and turn to the appendix for advice on résumés and interviews.

✴ Pay attention! Things can happen quickly. You should be changing the scenery or handing the prop to the actor before the director even asks you.

✴ Do a thorough job. Everything you do contributes to the overall quality of the performance.

## *Reality* Check

Grips, stagehands, and set-up workers do all the heavy, unglamorous work in theater. The work can be stressful and the salary irregular. However, you do get to work in an exciting, creative environment.

# *Some Other Jobs to Think About*

* Handicraftsperson. Instead of moving the scenery and props, why not make them?
* Camera operator. Camera operators are an important part of shooting any film or TV program.
* Electrician. Why not learn to operate the lights instead of setting them up? Electricians are the ones in charge of the lights themselves, and as union members, they have more job security.

# *How You Can Move Up*

* Become a designer. Many stage designers started on the bottom as stagehands.
* Become a director. Give expression to your own creative energies.
* Learn a trade. Skilled workers such as carpenters and electricians are indispensable to theatrical production.

## Web Sites to Surf

**Life as a Stagehand.** Read one man's tale of life behind the scenes.
http://www.flyingmoose.org/stage/stage.htm

**IATSE 80.** The Motion Picture Studio Grips' Union
http://www.iatselocal80.org

Work in an exciting industry

# TV/Film Camera Operator

Make a living doing something you love

Help create TV shows and movies

# TV/Film Camera Operator

Americans watch around 28 hours of TV a week and spend 12 hours at the movies each year. Yet some of the most important people in the TV and film industry are never seen on camera—because they're the ones running the camera itself! TV and film camera operators are in charge of capturing the action in front of the camera, no matter whether it's actors performing parts in a movie or real-life happenings such as professional sports, news events, and interviews for documentaries. Other TV and film camera operators work shooting everything from soap commercials to wars. There are about 28,000 TV and film camera operators working today in the United States.

## Is This Job for You?

To find out if being a TV or film camera operator is right for you, read each of the following questions and answer "Yes" or "No."

| | | | |
|---|---|---|---|
| Yes | No | **1.** | Are you a team player? |
| Yes | No | **2.** | Do you have a good artistic "eye?" |
| Yes | No | **3.** | Do you take directions well? |
| Yes | No | **4.** | Are you good with technology? |
| Yes | No | **5.** | Are you physically strong? |
| Yes | No | **6.** | Can you work long or irregular hours? |
| Yes | No | **7.** | Do you work well under pressure? |
| Yes | No | **8.** | Are you willing to start at the bottom? |
| Yes | No | **9.** | Can you move to where a job is, if necessary? |
| Yes | No | **10.** | Do you have good communications skills? |

If you answered "Yes" to most of these questions, you may have the essential skills for a career as a TV or film camera operator. To find out more about this job, read on.

## Let's Talk Money

The number of TV or film camera operators will grow about as fast as average through 2014. However, there is a lot of competition for jobs in this high-stress and demanding, yet very desirable, industry.

## *Let's Talk Trends*

The median income for TV or film camera operators is $37,610 per year, but can vary between $15,730 and $76,100, depending on your seniority and who you work for. Many are freelancers whose earnings change considerably from year to year.

# *What You'll Do*

The TV or film camera operator's job starts long before the director calls "Action!" Much of the magic of show business is planning—positioning the cameras, getting the lighting just right, and deciding when you'll be zooming in for a close-up and when you'll be pulling back for a long shot. You'll be working closely with the director, the sound and light equipment operators, and the "talent"—the people who will appear on camera. Of course, that's only if you're working in a studio. The places where a TV or film camera operator might work are as varied as the places where exciting and interesting things happen. You might find yourself doing everything from covering the opening of a new mini-mall to running through a war zone.

One thing doesn't change, though: The job of the TV or film camera operator is to capture images. In order to do this, you'll need a good sense of timing, as well as good hand-eye coordination to operate the camera. You'll also need to pay attention to the instructions of the director or producer. They will have very clear ideas of what they want the finished product to look like, and it's your job to help them accomplish this.

TV and film camera operators use many different kinds of cameras, from small handheld cameras to large ones mounted on crane arms. However, digital cameras are being used more and more frequently. Digital video is not only easier to edit, but can save money by not needing film, which is expensive both to buy and develop. They also tend to be smaller and easier to carry. What this means is that TV and film camera operators of the future will have to be comfortable with computers and digital editing programs.

# *Who You'll Work For*

✴ TV production companies
✴ Movie studios

✴ Local TV stations

✴ Production companies

## *Where You'll Work*

Most openings for TV and film camera operator jobs are in Los Angeles or New York, since these cities are where most movies, television shows, and commercials are shot. However, there are openings everywhere, since local TV news always needs camera operators. Major news organizations are also based in other cities. CNN, for instance, is headquartered in Atlanta, Georgia. TV commercials are also shot around the country.

The hours and workplaces for a TV or film camera operator can be very irregular. While TV and film camera operators employed by TV stations, called *studio camera operators,* usually work five-day, 40-hour weeks, this can vary widely depending on production schedules. Film camera operators, also called *cinematographers,* may have to travel widely to shoot on location. They may work 12- to 14-hour days on one project for weeks on end, and then have no work for a month or two. News camera operators, also called *electronic news gathering (ENG) operators,* may have to be available on short notice to fly to distant places. They may have to quickly edit their footage themselves for immediate broadcast. Their work can also be dangerous, especially if they cover wars or natural disasters.

The sorts of cameras used by people in this profession vary widely. You might have a camera light enough to be carried in one hand, or one that you need a crane to move. Some TV and film camera operators use specialized cameras, such as Steadicams (made by Tiffen) and those used to shoot special effects or animation.

## *What You Can Do Now*

✴ Assemble a "reel," or sample tape, of work you've done. This can showcase your shooting and editing skills.

✴ Volunteer or intern. This will help you meet people who can help you get entry-level jobs.

✴ Take classes. There are many filmmaking programs, and though you don't need a formal degree to be a camera operator, employers may want to know that you know what you're doing.

# The Inside Scoop: Q&A

**Stephan Ahonen**
**TV camera operator**
**Minneapolis, Minnesota**

**Q:** *How did you get your job?*

**A:** It's all about networking, knowing people who know people and making sure the people who hire crews know who you are. Volunteering for cable access or something like a large megaplex church that does a lot of video is a good way to meet people who may have connections that will get you an entry-level position on a crew somewhere. Internships don't really get you working on a TV crew, in my experience, since they're mostly geared toward four-year-degree-in-journalism types who want to produce or appear on camera.

**Q:** *What do you like best about your job?*

**A:** The challenge, the creativity, and the feeling you get when you're working on a live production that flows absolutely smoothly because you're working with a great team of professionals. If you're a musician, it's a feeling akin to taking part in a great improvised jam session, only much more expensive.

**Q:** *What's the most challenging part of your job?*

**A:** It's a 10-hour day, minimum. On your feet, lots of lifting and carrying. The pressure, too—it's live television, so there are no do-overs. Either you get it right the first time or people know you screwed up. People at home may not know it's you personally, but the person who hired you sure will. That's why you have to spend a lot of time working your way up, because when a million people are watching you, there can't be any possibility of a mistake.

**Q:** *What are the keys to success as a TV or film camera operator?*

**A:** Common sense, people skills, networking, creativity, intimate familiarity with the sport or other subject matter you're shooting. Actual technical proficiency at running the equipment pretty much takes care of itself through the practice you get in the process of working your way up. You won't get hired for bigger gigs until you demonstrate your proficiency on smaller ones.

# *Your Typical Day*

Here are the highlights of a typical day for a TV or film camera operator.

✓ **Start early.** Your phone rings at 5 a.m. A client you worked for last month is shooting a TV commercial today, and the regular camera operator is sick. Are you interested in some work? Oh, yes—you have an hour to get to the set.

✓ **Hurry up and wait.** The talent doesn't have to be on the set until 10 a.m., but you've already spent the past four hours setting up the cameras. Unfortunately, this is a diaper commercial, which means the "talent" is a pair of two-year-old twin girls—which means you have to wait around while the director gets them just in the right spot, tries to get them to smile, or swaps them when they begin crying or need a diaper change.

✓ **Finish late.** Long after the talent goes home, you're still at work, spending hours getting shot after shot of a box of diapers for the commercial. You leave work exhausted—but with a large paycheck!

# *What Training You'll Need*

Though you don't need a college degree to be a TV or film camera operator, training never hurts. Many high schools have audio-visual clubs and video labs that you can practice with. Also consider getting a camera and some editing software to practice on your own. You can also read trade magazines to learn the latest techniques and tips.

Another way to learn the basics is through an entry-level job, summer employment, or an internship. There you will learn to set up lights and shots, make adjustments to cameras, and decide what to photograph. There are also many filmmaking schools that can teach you the basics of the trade—everything from lighting and setting up shots to developing the finished film. Such schools can be expensive, however, and completing a course is no guarantee of getting a job.

Since computers are becoming more and more important in the TV and film industries, it is important to be computer-literate. Learn to use editing software, and also learn how digital video is different from analog and from the various film stocks. Things can look very different on a computer than they do projected on a movie screen.

Finally, some of the things employers look for in a TV or film camera operator, such as a good artistic eye, creativity, and imagination, can't be taught. However, you need to be able to demonstrate these attributes. To this end, you should get as much practice as you can, and prepare a videotape or DVD of your work to show prospective employers.

## *How to Talk Like a Pro*

Here are a few words you'll hear as a TV or film camera operator:

✯ **Steadicam** Unlike other cameras, the Tiffen Steadicam is mounted on a harness. A special arm keeps it from shaking as the operator moves, resulting in a smooth shot.

✯ **Editor** The editor is the person who takes the raw footage shot by the camera operator and puts it together to tell a story.

✯ **ENG** "Electronic News Gathering." Industry shorthand for a sole reporter or a whole crew who transmit their stories via radio waves to the broadcast production studio.

## *How to Find a Job*

As has often been said, it's not just what you know, but who you know. The most important consideration employers look for in the TV and film industries is reputation. Reputation comes from people both knowing your work and knowing you as an experienced and reliable camera operator. If you want to work as a TV or film camera operator, then you should start making contacts in the industry right away. The people you meet may be able to get you jobs later on.

The other factor in the equation is experience. However, people who work for the TV and film industries tend to be film buffs and video "junkies" from a young age, and there are many ways for creative people to get experience: Start a public-access TV show with some friends. Work on an independent movie, or even make your own. Volunteer at a church or organization that does a lot of video work and look for summer jobs and internships. All of these are also good ways to meet people who can help you find jobs. Moreover, by giving expression to your creative energies, you can learn to become a skilled camera operator.

# Secrets for Success

See the suggestions below and turn to the appendix for advice on résumés and interviews.

- ⭐ Pay attention to directions. Remember, you're part of a team.
- ⭐ Be a people person. TV and film are highly social industries.
- ⭐ Consider moving to where the work is. There are more jobs in film and TV in big cities than there are in small towns.

# Reality Check

The TV and film industries are highly competitive. This means that not only is it difficult to get jobs, but because many TV and film camera operators are freelancers, you may go a long time between jobs.

# Some Other Jobs to Think About

- ⭐ Set dresser. When you've watched two people having dinner in a movie, have you ever wondered who put the plates on the tables? Guess what—it's the set dresser. This is one of the many behind-the-scenes jobs in the movie industry.
- ⭐ Sound technician. Sound technicians are to the ear what camera operators are to the eye. They are responsible for capturing the audio portion of the film or TV show.
- ⭐ Lighting technician. Cameras don't work unless they have light! Also, the quality of light can make a big difference in the finished product. The lighter's job is to make sure that everybody looks perfect.

# How You Can Move Up

- ⭐ Go big. Successful camera operators can move to bigger and bigger jobs. Eventually they can earn administrative positions, such as directors of photography.
- ⭐ Those who can, teach. If you're a successful camera operator, why not get a job at a technical school teaching other people to become camera operators?
- ⭐ Become a director. Consider making your own independent films and documentaries.

## Web Sites to Surf

**National Association of Broadcast Employees and Technicians.** This is the union for TV camera operators and other professionals. http://www.nabetcwa.org

**International Cinematographer's Guild.** This is the international union for people who operate cameras for movies, and the Web site features technical tips. http://www.cameraguild.com

# Phone/Cable Installer

Visit a variety of job sites

Work for a large company

Work outdoors and indoors

# *Phone/Cable* Installer

Though telephone systems have been around for more than a century and cable television since the late 1960s, the enormous growth of the Internet in the 1990s led to a demand for new communication infrastructure. Old-fashioned dial-up access was simply too slow for the new wealth of sound, pictures, and video. Some way had to be found to connect schools, homes, and businesses for the high-speed transmission of data. The answer was to use the already existing cable and phone lines to provide broadband access. Telecommunications jobs were suddenly in high demand, and installers found themselves connecting not just televisions but also computers. There are about 50 million broadband Internet users and 147,000 phone and cable installers in the United States today.

## *Is This Job for You?*

To find out if being a phone or cable installer is right for you, read each of the following questions and answer "Yes" or "No."

| Yes | No | **1.** | Can you follow directions precisely? |
|-----|-----|-----|-----|
| Yes | No | **2.** | Do you work well independently? |
| Yes | No | **3.** | Do you always play by the rules? |
| Yes | No | **4.** | Are you good with tools? |
| Yes | No | **5.** | Are you good at math and science? |
| Yes | No | **6.** | Are you good with computers? |
| Yes | No | **7.** | Do you have good communications skills? |
| Yes | No | **8.** | Do you have a driver's license? |
| Yes | No | **9.** | Can you see in color? |
| Yes | No | **10.** | Are you in good physical shape? |

If you answered "Yes" to most of these questions, you might want to consider a career as a phone or cable installer. To find out more about these jobs, read on.

## *What You'll Do*

As their job title implies, phone and cable installers connect, repair, and maintain telecommunications lines to homes, schools, and businesses. Doing this, however, is not as easy as it sounds. Because cable and phone companies have many customers, they tightly schedule appointments to connect services. It is important to do your job quickly and well, because people may have to take time away from work or school in order to let you into their houses.

When arriving on a job site, you must first locate the interface between the customer's property and the main cable. This is the cable that runs underground or on utility poles back to the distribution center. For telephone service, this will be a wall jack; for cable, this will be a coaxial cable. If no connection exists, you may have to create one. Some homes use satellite dishes instead of cable for their connections.

The next task is to connect the home or business to the network, which may require joining, or splicing, cables. If wires need to be run through a living or work space, you will need to run them carefully so that they are out of the way. An authorization code must often be called in to the main office to start the "flow" of data. Then you must make sure that the telephone or cable box is properly connected to the system, and the box, in turn, is connected to the computer or television. Computers must often have the proper software and settings installed. Finally, you must test the system, explain to the customer how to use it, and then speed off to the next appointment.

## *Who* You'll Work For

* Phone companies
* Cable companies
* Building equipment carriers

## *Where* You'll Work

Because utilities such as telephone and cables can cause a lot of disruption when the main lines are laid through city streets, governments grant limited monopolies to the companies who own these

### Let's Talk Money

The median income for phone and cable installers is $19.39 per hour, but can vary between $10.96 and $28.56. Those working for wired telecommunications carriers, such as phone and cable companies, tend to make the most, and those working in utility construction, who install new lines, tend to make the least.

## Let's Talk Trends

The number of phone and cable installers will grow about as fast as the average for all occupations through 2014. Much of their work will consist of replacing old wiring with fiber-optic cable and expanding networks to meet demand. However, wireless technology is expected to make much of the old system obsolete.

systems. Most phone and cable installers, therefore, work for these big companies. Some also work for construction contractors and other companies who have an interest in wiring buildings.

The places where you may install phone or cable lines are as varied as the homes, businesses, and schools that need high-speed, modern communications. Within these places, you may also need to climb ladders, go up on roofs and balconies, or other hard-to-reach places where cables need to be spliced. You will sometimes have to lift heavy bales of cable or toolboxes.

Working as a phone or cable installer can be very hectic. You may have to deal with many customers in one day, and have little time to do each job. You may also have to deal with people who blame you for things that aren't your fault, such as utility outages. However, many people see dealing with many different people and not having to work in an office as one benefit of this job.

## *Your* Typical Day

Here are the highlights of a typical day for a cable installer.

✓ **Getting there is half the fun.** Today you will be installing a cable modem for a new tenant in a Manhattan apartment building. The first challenge, of course, is finding the address.

✓ **Dealing with the customers.** You find the building with little problem, but the customer is angry that you weren't there an hour ago. After she locks her overly friendly dog up in the bedroom, you get to work connecting the system to the main line—which, it turns out, means going up the fire escape to the roof of the building.

✓ **Testing it out.** The tester says that the line is functioning, but her computer still can't get on the Internet. After you adjust a few settings, everything is working fine. On to the next job!

## *What You Can Do Now*

✴ Learn how phone and cable systems work, and how computers connect to the Internet.

✴ Learn about electronics. A phone or cable system is much like an electric circuit.

✴ Pay attention in math and science classes. These teach the principles by which phone and cable systems work.

## *What Training You'll Need*

Most phone and cable installers are trained by the companies they work for. You may have to serve apprenticeships lasting one to three years. You may also have to attend training given by equipment suppliers or other companies. Some certification programs are offered through unions and other organizations. For instance, the Society of Cable Television Engineers has a certification program for cable installers and repairers offered through local SCTE chapters.

There are also trade and technical programs, lasting one year or more, that are often offered by local community colleges and trade and vocational schools in cooperation with utility companies. Such courses will teach you about electricity, electronics, communications technology. Many are hands-on, offering practical experience as well. Meanwhile, pay attention in high school. Math, science, and computer courses all teach you the essential skills you will need later.

Some important assets are a driver's license, color vision, and mechanical ability. Because you will need to get from job site to job site, it is essential to be able to drive. Because many wires and cables are color-coded, color-blind people can have difficulty distinguishing between them. Because you will need to connect, separate, and splice cables, it is important to be good with tools.

## *How to Talk Like a Pro*

Here are a few words you'll hear as a phone or cable installer:

✴ **DSL** Digital Subscriber Line—high-speed Internet access through a phone line.

✴ **Coaxial cable** An electrical cable surrounded by an insulator, used to carry a high-frequency signal.

✴ **IP** Internet Protocol, a unique numerical address that lets computers talk to one another over the Internet.

# The Inside Scoop: Q&A

**Jim Martin**
**Cable installer**
**Jacksonville, Florida**

**Q:** *How did you get your job?*

**A:** Nine years ago, I did what people used to do—look at the want ads in the paper. Two months after I sent my résumé (and had practically forgotten about it), I had my first interview. A month later, I was in the cable television industry.

**Q:** *What do you like best about your job?*

**A:** I am challenged daily to explain technical things to non-technical people. In many cases, you have to figure out how to get a person to understand what you are saying and then deliver instructions to them so that they can understand and retain it. I love the look a person gets when they "get" what I am explaining to them.

**Q:** *What's the most challenging part of your job?*

**A:** I find it difficult to check and make sure that every channel, every computer, and every phone is working 100 percent correctly. This seems like it would be easy to do, but when you are dealing with four TVs, three computers, and five phones, it can be difficult. Not to mention the wiring, the education of the customer, and the little challenges that go with adding tons of wiring to a house. For example, crawling through an attic on a hot day and going under a house after a heavy rain.

**Q:** *What are the keys to success as a cable installer?*

**A:** In my job, it is critical to fix it right the first time. When we have to go to a job again and again, it wastes my company's money and steals important time away from the customer. Paying attention to detail, even for difficult service calls and installations, is very important. You have to be flexible. You can't take five hours to do a job that statistics show usually takes 30 minutes. Finally, you must keep everything you work with organized. I work out of a van and if things get out of place, it takes me time to hunt them down. It's fairly easy to let it go and let it get dirty, but it really hurts you when you need to find that one piece of equipment.

# How to Find a Job

Since there is usually only one phone or cable company for an area, it is easy to know where to inquire about job openings. Call or e-mail to ask about training programs. Generally, the department you will want to speak to is Human Resources. The company may give you further tips for what qualifications they look for in applicants. Phone and cable companies often advertise for installers in local newspapers and on their Web sites.

You may also want to ask local trade and vocational schools about their training programs. Such schools often have placement programs with local utility companies.

# Secrets for Success

See the suggestions below and turn to the appendix for advice on résumés and interviews.

* Always be polite and friendly to the customer. A positive attitude is infectious.
* Take the time to do the job right. There's no going back on a tight schedule.

# Reality Check

Phone and cable installers often have tight schedules and high workloads. They are also dependent on one company for their jobs. Finally, the telecommunications field is changing rapidly and some skills could be obsolete in a few years, so look for ways to learn new skills that will keep you in demand once you embark on your career.

# Some Other Jobs to Think About

* Electrician. Electricians also deal with wires and cables, but are skilled laborers who make good salaries.
* Line installer and repairer. These workers install and repair high-voltage cables. This job can be dangerous, but pays very well.
* Computer network technician. Help to maintain and expand computer networks.

# *How You Can Move Up*

⋆ Become a manager. In time, you may be able to supervise other cable or phone installers.

⋆ Get additional training. The more you know, the more jobs will open up to you, such as maintaining the main lines that run to the central offices—a responsibility that offers steady and well-paying work.

⋆ Go back to school. More advanced managerial positions generally require a college degree.

## Web Sites to Surf

**SCTE.** The Society of Cable Telecommunications Engineers, offering training and advocacy. http://www.scte.org/international.cfm

**How Telephones Work.** An explanation from Howstuffworks.com. http://www.electronics.howstuffworks.com/telephone.htm

Meet creative people

# Photographer's Assistant

Work in an exciting industry

See your work in print

# *Great Careers*

# *Photographer's Assistant*

Louis Daguerre's invention of practical photography in 1826 gave rise to a whole new art form. Soon photography was replacing painting as the way people wanted to have their portraits made, how they remembered the past, and how they saw the world. With the advent of new printing methods in the twentieth century, photographs could easily and cheaply be printed in books and magazines, and photography became an even bigger business. Today photographers do everything from taking baby pictures at shopping malls to shooting supermodels in the latest fashions. Photographer's assistants help photographers in all they do, from carrying equipment to setting up lights to working with models. Usually, photographer's assistants are aspiring photographers themselves. There are about 129,000 professional photographers working in this highly competitive field in the United States today.

## *Is This Job for You?*

To find out if being a photographer's assistant is right for you, read each of the following questions and answer "Yes" or "No."

| | | | |
|---|---|---|---|
| *Yes* | *No* | **1.** | Do you love photography? |
| *Yes* | *No* | **2.** | Do you work well with all sorts of people? |
| *Yes* | *No* | **3.** | Do you have an artistic eye for color and light? |
| *Yes* | *No* | **4.** | Can you carry heavy loads? |
| *Yes* | *No* | **5.** | Are you very patient? |
| *Yes* | *No* | **6.** | Are you good with computers and technology? |
| *Yes* | *No* | **7.** | Do you pay attention to details? |
| *Yes* | *No* | **8.** | Are you knowledgeable about photography equipment? |
| *Yes* | *No* | **9.** | Can you follow directions? |
| *Yes* | *No* | **10.** | Do you mind starting at the bottom? |

If you answered "Yes" to most of these questions, you may have the talent to pursue a career as a photographer's assistant. To find out more about this job, read on.

## Let's Talk Money

The U.S. Department of Labor does not keep statistics on photographer's assistants, but the median income for salaried photographers is $26,080 and ranges from $15,000 to $54,180. News organizations and scientific companies tend to pay at the higher end of the scale. Photographers who work for a salary also tend to make more money than freelancers, who make up about 50 percent of professional photographers. Photographer's assistants tend to make much less. In fact, many work as volunteers for the experience.

# What You'll Do

Since photographer's assistants tend to be aspiring photographers themselves, they should know the elements of photography. Most important is good light. To achieve a certain look, a photographer may need a certain sort of light, such as a diffused glow or a spotlight that casts strong shadows. A large part of the photographer's assistant's job is setting up lights. The photographer's assistant should know—or be willing to learn—how to set up light boxes, lamps, reflectors, and other equipment to achieve these effects, as well as how to use light meters. Part of the job also includes carrying and connecting transformers and generators for the lights, as well as other equipment.

Being organized is also very important. During a shoot, you will hand cameras to the photographer, change the film in cameras, put spent film into canisters, and mark down what is on the film. For larger shoots, you might do anything and everything needed. For instance, you may coordinate schedules with hairdressers and costumers, tell models when they are needed on the set, take care of paperwork, make sure releases are signed, and arrange catering. You might even videotape the proceedings. If you assist a photographer who works in news media, you will not work in such a controlled environment. You may have to carry heavy equipment for long distances. You may also have to travel to distant or even dangerous locations.

Finally, you should remember that you may be doing a lot of things that aren't in your job description. Especially in high-living places like New York, photographer's assistants tend to become all-around valets. You might find yourself picking up dry cleaning as well as loading film. In exchange for your labor, though, you should be learning the art of photography in an exciting and creative environment. However, keep in mind that where you intern affects where you find work: If you intern in the New York fashion industry, then that is where your contacts will be.

## Who You'll Work For

✴ Freelance photographers
✴ Photography studios
✴ News organizations

## Where You'll Work

Photographer's assistants sometimes have the luxury of working in comfortable, well-lit, and climate-controlled studios. However, you may have to travel to all sorts of interesting sites, including showrooms, dance clubs, or tropical islands. A fine art photographer might shoot pictures of animals in a zoo or bodybuilders in the gym—anywhere that takes their fancy. A news photographer might travel to anywhere there is news. Some photographers and photographer's assistants find work shooting pictures for catalogs, Web sites, scientific journals, and research facilities. For instance, large clothing chains often maintain an image library of products.

Most photographer's assistants work in New York, Los Angeles, or other major cities. As the media and entertainment centers for the United States and the world, these are natural focus points for aspiring photographers. Sometimes the creative energy at a shoot and having to deal with so many demanding people can create a lot of stress. The ability to remain calm, polite, and effective in all situations is very important for photographer's assistants.

### Let's Talk Trends

According to the Department of Labor, the number of photographers (and photographer's assistants) is expected to grow about as fast as average through 2014. However, competition for these jobs is fierce. The large number of people entering the field will keep wages low and opportunities scarce for all but the most talented and in-demand photographers.

Hours can vary. While some jobs, such as shooting products for a catalog, may have a regular 9-to-5, 40-hour workweek, most do not. Like all artists, photographers can keep strange hours. Some shoots will take place during the day, some at night. Some photographers will work weekends, while some won't. Sometimes, shoots are limited by the subjects' or the studio's schedule. If a particular model, actor, or athlete is available only on Tuesday evenings, that is when you will have to work. You will need to be flexible and available whenever you are needed.

A photographer's assistant's job is not easy. Keeping track of everything and dealing with so many problems so the photographer can concentrate on his or her job is not for the faint of heart! Many feel, however, that the nature of the job makes up for these inconveniences. You will get to meet and interact with interesting and, occasionally, famous people and work with the latest and best photography equipment.

## *Your Typical Day*

Here are the highlights of a typical day for a photographer's assistant.

✓ **Lights!** Today the photographer you work for will be shooting a fashion spread for a well-known magazine. Hours before the models arrive, though, you're on the set setting up the lights, loading the cameras, and making sure the food arrives.

✓ **Camera!** The next 14 hours are a blur of work. As soon as one roll of film is shot, you reload the camera and hand it off. Another assistant takes the film, writes down what's on it, and safely stores it.

✓ **Action!** After a long day, you're tired and want to go home. But there's still more to be done. The lights and equipment need to be broken down, and the studio needs to be closed up.

## *What You Can Do Now*

✴ Learn all you can about photography. If you can, ask a professional photographer if you can observe a shoot, so that you know what goes on.

✴ Try to meet professional photographers. One handshake is worth any number of e-mails.

# The Inside Scoop: Q&A

**Rosie McCobb**
**Photographer**
**Brooklyn, New York**

**Q:** *How did you get your job?*

**A:** I started out applying for an entry-level job as an archival photographer at a retail store's corporate archive, and that enabled me to get enough experience to get another, better paying job as a product photographer for a fashion retail Web site. For my current job, I saw an ad on Craigslist for a product photographer for a women's clothing company, and I applied, sending them my résumé and a link to my portfolio. I was told by my employers that they called me first because I had worked at the same company as one of the owners. This helped immensely, because they got over 400 responses.

**Q:** *What do you like best about your job?*

**A:** The freedom, physically and socially. I don't have to go to an office and sit behind a desk all day, which I love. I also don't have to participate in any corporate or office politics, which is also great. At my current job, because it's a new company, I also get to interact directly with the owners and have a lot of input about the Web site and marketing of their Web business.

**Q:** *What's the most challenging part of your job?*

**A:** Negotiating for things that I need—whether that be requesting more equipment to get the job done, or trying to come to an agreement about exactly what my job entails and how much money I will be paid for my work. A lot of people in business don't understand the amount of time, equipment, and money that goes into making good photographs.

**Q:** *What are the keys to success as a photographer?*

**A:** Having good communication skills, good organization skills, and a good head for business. Of course, you need to be able to do the kind of work you're applying for or putting in a bid for, but being

*(Continued on next page)*

*(continued from previous page)*

a good businessperson is equally, if not more important, in the big picture. Also, you have to be a patient person, and able to deal with lots of different kinds of people, some of whom are stressed out or overworked when they are calling you.

✻ Build a portfolio of your own work. Prospective employers will want some assurance that you know what you're doing. A Web site is an excellent place to display your work.

## *What Training You'll Need*

The entire purpose of working as a photographer's assistant is to gain experience in photography. The job can, in many ways, be thought of as an apprenticeship. However, this does not mean that you should not seek to educate yourself. Before looking for a job as a photographer's assistant, it is important to know a lot about all sorts of cameras, both digital and film, as well as photographic equipment. Working in a camera store can be valuable training, as can reading books on photography and subscribing to photographic magazines. A good understanding of art history and symbolism is also helpful.

Because of the increasing popularity of digital photography (even pictures taken on film are often scanned when used for professional production), you will need to be good with computers. The industry standard for retouching blemishes, adjusting colors and light, and many other applications is Adobe's Photoshop. Learn how to use this important computer program!

Attending trade and vocational schools, as well as community college courses, can help you learn the technical aspects of photography. There are also schools, such as the School of Visual Arts in New York City, that offer everything from evening courses to degrees in fine arts such as photography. However, you won't get as much "real world" experience in such places as you would working as an assistant and shooting your own pictures. Furthermore, you will not be making the contacts you need to further your career. For this reason, many working artists consider formal education in photography to be unnecessary.

For more on how to begin as a photographer's assistant, see "How to Find a Job," below.

# How to Talk Like a Pro

Here are a few words you'll hear as a photographer's assistant:

⭐ **Transparency** The professional name for a photographic "slide," as you would use in a slide projector. Slides generally have better color reproduction and last longer.

⭐ **Back lighting** Placing the light source so the subject is between the camera and the light.

⭐ **Light meter** A very useful device that tells you exactly how much light you have to work with. Because the human eye adjusts to light levels, it can be difficult to tell how what you see will look on film. The light meter accurately reads the light levels.

# How to Find a Job

Finding a job can be the hardest part of being a photographer's assistant. Very rarely, newspapers or (more usually) online forums such as Craigslist (http://www.craigslist.org) will have help-wanted ads. However, if you are going to succeed in photography, you are going to have to take matters into your own hands. Go out of your way to build a portfolio, attend gallery openings, meet professional photographers, and otherwise try to enter the world of professional photography.

The first and most important thing is that any inquiry to become a photographer's assistant should be accompanied by a thoroughly proofread and artistically well-designed résumé. Building a résumé can take time, and writing a résumé is an art in itself, but if done well, it will indicate not only that you are a hard worker but that you pay attention to detail and have an artist's eye. Indicating in your query letter or e-mail that you are available any time, day or night, can help, as many professional photographers keep erratic schedules.

Finally, network. Get to know professional photographers who might hire you. Many photographers prefer to work with people they already know and have a relationship with. Social networking Web sites such as MySpace (http://www.myspace.com) are one way of doing this, but even better is introducing yourself at public events. Additionally, a Web site of your own will help to show your own photography to prospective clients and employers. Since many professionals already have assistants they work with regularly, offer to be an intern or second assistant, helping their helper. Again, the important thing is building relationships.

All of this takes a lot of time, and pays very little money. You may need to take on a second or even third job in addition to working as a photographer's assistant, especially in expensive cities such as New York, San Francisco, and Los Angeles. While you might want to start in a less expensive city such as Chicago or Minneapolis, the best opportunities are on the coasts—and remember, persistence is the key to success.

# *Secrets for Success*

See the suggestions below and turn to the appendix for advice on résumés and interviews.

* Photography, like all the arts, is a highly social profession. Being a "people person" is essential.
* Be organized! The photographer's assistant's real job is to be the one who knows where everything is and what happens next.

# *Reality Check*

Photography is a very difficult industry to get ahead in. Photographer's assistants work long hours and are not paid very much. Very few can make ends meet by working in this industry alone.

# *Some Other Jobs to Think About*

* Graphic designer. Like photographers, graphic designers must have a good "eye," but tend to work alone.
* TV/film camera operator. The skills needed for this job are much the same as for photography, but the work can be more steady.
* Photographic process workers. If you love photography, why not work in a developing studio? High-end professional camera stores require good, knowledgeable workers.

# *How* You Can Move Up

✳ Sell your work. Most photographer's assistants are themselves photographers. The more you show your work to people, no matter if it's in an art gallery, a restaurant, or your living room, the more people will know your name.

✳ Sell yourself. If you have experience, make connections, get jobs, and sell your work!

✳ Sell out. Working in an office as a picture editor digitally retouching other people's photographs or shooting products for a catalog or Web site is not glamorous, but it does pay the bills.

## *Web Sites to Surf*

**ASMP.** Perhaps the best guide to entering the business on the Web. On the Web site of the American Society of Media Photographers http://www.asmp.org/commerce/photog_assist.php

**APA.** The Advertising Photographers of America, a trade organization for professional photographers.  http://www.apanational.com

Discover the joys of performing

# Singer, Dancer, Performer

Succeed in an exciting and challenging career

Sing, dance, and make people happy

# Singer, Dancer, Performer

While professional performers have been around since ancient Greece, modern culture has raised entertainment to never-before-seen heights. Today performers in genres from heavy metal to opera to hip-hop to ballet to Broadway are considered celebrities and role models. Others, such as members of symphony orchestra, don't experience the limelight but make a good living working behind the scenes. However, 40 percent of professional musicians work only part-time, and those who do manage to "make it" often struggle for years. There are about 249,000 working singers and musicians and 38,000 professional dancers in the United States today. About 250,000 people work in all arts, entertainment, and recreation jobs in Canada.

## Is This Job for You?

To find out if being a singer, dancer, or performer is right for you, read each of the following questions and answer "Yes" or "No."

| | | | |
|---|---|---|---|
| Yes | No | **1.** | Do people believe you have real talent? |
| Yes | No | **2.** | Do you have a great need to be on stage? |
| Yes | No | **3.** | Do you believe in yourself? |
| Yes | No | **4.** | Are you an excellent networker and people person? |
| Yes | No | **5.** | Are you willing to work as hard as you need to achieve your goals? |
| Yes | No | **6.** | Do you have an excellent sense of pitch and rhythm? |
| Yes | No | **7.** | Can you work well as part of a team? |
| Yes | No | **8.** | Can you perform in a great variety of situations? |
| Yes | No | **9.** | Do you have stage presence? |
| Yes | No | **10.** | Do you practice every day? |

If you answered "Yes" to most of these questions, you might be happy in a career as a singer, dancer, or performer. To find out more about these jobs, read on.

## What You'll Do

Singers and other performers sing, play instruments, and/or compose music. This music can be performed live or recorded for later playback, for instance, as background for a TV commercial. The job is

## Let's Talk Money

According to the U.S. Department of Labor, the median income for musicians, singers, and related workers is $17.85 per hour, but can vary between $6.47 and $53.59. According to the American Federation of Musicians, the minimum salaries in a major orchestra could range from $700 to $2,080 per week. Dancers earn a median of $8.54 per hour, but could earn as little as $5.87 or as much as $21.59. Those working in performance troupes tended to earn at the high end of the scale. Of course, "stars" such as best-selling artists, opera singers, and prima ballerinas can make significantly more. Much employment is short-term.

as varied as the types of music people listen to. Vocalists may perform in any style from hip-hop to gospel to jazz to Broadway to heavy metal. Instrumentalists play anything from antique harpsichords to a DJ's turntables. A rock or heavy metal band can have anywhere from three members (usually guitar, bass, and drums) to eight or more (ska bands, for instance, usually add a horn section), while some styles do not require musical accompaniment. Rappers, for instance, may simply use a prerecorded backing track. Classical musicians range from opera singers to orchestra members to composers, though jobs in classical music usually require attending a *conservatory* or other formal music-education program. *Studio musicians* do not perform, but contribute to other artists' albums or provide backing tracks for other performers. *Musical theater,* such as Broadway shows, generally requires a combination of singing, dancing, and acting skills. *Composers* and *arrangers* generally must know how to read and write musical notation.

Dancers can work in any genre from ballet to hip-hop. *Choreographers* are usually experienced dancers who design and arrange dances for others.

## Where You'll Work

Generally, singers, dancers, and performers perform on nights and weekends, but the job requires far more time commitment than merely performing. Dancers, for instance, may spend eight hours a day or more in practice. Most good singers also take lessons and work with voice coaches and other trainers. Recording an album, for instance, can be a long and difficult task.

Performance venues vary widely. Depending on what kind of music you perform, you might find yourself anywhere from a majestic opera or ballet hall to a smoky nightclub or raucous bar to a comfortable recording studio. Secondhand smoke can be an occupational hazard in some places. Singers and musicians can find work in many other places besides these venues, of course. People having social events such as weddings, bar mitzvahs, and sweet sixteen parties often hire singers and bands to entertain guests. Cruise ships, which often feature live entertainment, are another large source of employment for singers, dancers, and performers. However, most jobs, like the arts and music industry, tend to be concentrated in cities such as New York, Los Angeles, Nashville, San Francisco, Las Vegas, and Toronto. Auditions for jobs are often held in these cities even if the job itself will be with a touring company or performing in a revue at a tropical vacation resort.

The main difficulty of working as a singer, dancer, or performer is that many jobs pay very little, or are only part-time, or are only short-term. Few offer benefits; if you get a sore throat or pull a hamstring, that can be the end of the job. Long-term unemployment is a distinct possibility. Even for successful singers, dancers, and performers, the pressures of touring can be great.

## Who You'll Work For

✴ Orchestras
✴ Record companies
✴ Dance troupes
✴ Bars and nightclubs
✴ Cruise ships and entertainment companies
✴ Self-employment

### Let's Talk Trends

The number of singers, dancers, and performers will grow about as fast as the average through 2014. However, the field is extremely competitive, with many musicians competing for comparatively little work. Many leave the field because they lack the discipline or are not willing or able to endure the long periods of unemployment.

# *Your Typical Day*

Here are the highlights of a typical day for a singer working on a cruise ship.

✔ **Wake-up call.** The previous night's show ended at 1 a.m., and you're still tired and groggy when you wake up at noon. This cruise is no vacation for you!

✔ **Rehearsal.** After a quick breakfast (being careful not to eat anything that will aggravate your already sore throat), it's off to the ship's theater. The show's director has some new ideas he wants to try out.

✔ **Sing your heart out.** The evening's entertainment begins at 11 p.m. For two hours you sing some of the greatest show tunes of the twentieth century for a crowd of appreciative middle-aged vacationers. Finally, at the end of the night, you collapse in bed, tired and happy.

# *What You Can Do Now*

✯ Practice. Then practice some more.

✯ Audition for a troupe, form a band, find an open-mike night, or otherwise get experience performing.

✯ Try to meet people who can help you in your career. Both the dance scene and the music industry are highly social.

# *What Training You'll Need*

Most singers, dancers, and performers "hear the call" at a very early age. The most important thing is to get as much practice and experience in music or dance as you can. Various sorts of training are available. While many professionals offer private lessons, there are also classes you can take in high school. Some high schools, such as New York City's High School for the Performing Arts, are, in fact, devoted to music and dance. Extracurricular activities such as marching bands, student shows, and choral groups are both fun and great training. Other organizations, such as churches, community theaters, choirs, and other not-for-profit groups, can also be great experiences. Don't be afraid to take the initiative: Forming your own band and playing music is one way to get appreciation for your music and

# The Inside Scoop: Q&A

**Charlette Jones**
**Singer, dancer, and performer**
**Uniondale, Illinois**

**Q:** *How did you get your job?*

**A:** I got the job by walking into a restaurant and they were having an open-mike session and no one was there singing and everything was over. So I talked the guy into giving him a sample and there were a few people left in the restaurant and when I was singing, one of the guys was so moved he had tears in his eyes. They saw how the people responded and they offered me a job.

**Q:** *What do you like best about your job?*

**A:** I get to do something that I love to do and would even do it for free if I didn't have bills to pay.

**Q:** *What's the most challenging part of your job?*

**A:** Laryngitis. I couldn't even whisper. I never want to go through it again. The other challenging part is a singer needs a lot of rest. I need my own place where I can rest. Artists don't sleep when everyone else sleeps. I may sleep from 1 a.m. to 9 or 10 in the morning . . . so the most challenging thing is needing a place to stay where my rest is not interrupted.

**Q:** *What are the keys to success as a singer, dancer, or performer?*

**A:** Believe in yourself.

talent. However, venues can be limited. Many nightclubs and bars don't allow anyone under 21 to enter, including musicians.

If you are intending to become a singer or musician, you should also learn to read and write musical notation, as well as musical theory, as these can be invaluable aids to a career. While careers in classical music generally require formal training in a college program or conservatory, there are many other ways to gain knowledge and experience. Playing with older musicians, for instance, is one way to pick up new tricks. Another way is reading music magazines, which can keep you knowledgeable about techniques and equipment used by the pros. Some also offer transcriptions of popular songs. You learn a lot by actually working as a singer or musician—how to follow time changes, how to have "stage presence," how to present yourself to a potential record label. Listening to musicians whose work you'd like to emulate and going to see them perform live can help greatly. Always look, listen, and keep your ears open.

Dancers follow a long and arduous road to success. Most begin their training at an early age and practice daily. Patience, perseverance, and a willingness to work hard are essential qualities. You need to both be able to face rejection and to work as part of a team. Some qualities, like rhythm, grace, a feel for music, and the ability to heal quickly from physical injuries can't be taught.

## How to Talk Like a Pro

Here are a few words you'll hear as a dancer, singer, or performer:

⋆ **Cover** "Covering" is a term for playing a song (usually a well-known one) written by someone else. A "cover band" plays exclusively covers.

⋆ **Monitor** Musicians on stage, particularly those using public-address systems, can't hear what the crowd hears. A monitor is a special speaker to allow them to hear their own music.

⋆ **Touring company** Many singers, dancers, and performers, especially those in musical theater, find jobs in touring companies that play around the country.

## How to Find a Job

Being a singer, dancer, or performer, like pursuing any career in the performing arts, requires you to be very social. The best and most successful professionals are masters of networking. Madonna, for instance, first gained exposure from famous New York DJs such as Mark Kamins. You will need to build an extensive network of contacts among club owners, choreographers, theater company managers, agents, entertainment lawyers, and reviewers. All of these are people who can help you get work and introduce your work to new audiences.

Most jobs with dance companies, troupes, orchestras, or shows usually require an audition of some sort. Casting calls go out in trade publications such as *Billboard* or *Variety* or on online forums such as Craigslist (http://www.craigslist.org). Generally, you will have to dance, sing, or play a piece of music.

Sometimes, bars or clubs hold open auditions for bands and singers. Some will even allow unknowns to play. The influential New York punk band the Ramones, for instance, were completely unknown when they played their first gig at the famous CBGB club in Manhattan's East Village. However, venues such as these are becoming much harder to find. Most clubs want to know that you will bring in a paying audience. Some are even "pay-to-play," where you will have to front money in order to perform in hopes of making it back through door covers.

## *Secrets for Success*

See the suggestions below and turn to the appendix for advice on résumés and interviews.

- ✦ It's very tempting to stay up all night socializing after a performance. Don't! The smoky air, physical stress, and lack of sleep will ruin your voice or dancing.
- ✦ Many people believe that agents are the key to contracts. Agents and managers are a dime a dozen—it's entertainment lawyers that have the record companies' ears.
- ✦ Moving to a major city is sometimes necessary. There are more people—and dance troupes, recording studios, and record executives—in Los Angeles than there are in Des Moines.
- ✦ Getting yourself out there is the most important thing. Make demo CDs, make your friends and your friends' friends attend your shows, and make some noise on the Internet.

## *Reality Check*

Many young people have dreams about making it big as dancers or in the music industry. In reality, the world is structured like a tournament. Many, many people work very hard and are very poorly paid, while a very few "winners" gain any measure of success. Be sure to have skills you can fall back on.

## *Some Other Jobs to Think About*

✴ Music instrument repairs and sales. To earn a steady paycheck, many musicians learn to repair and sell musical equipment.

✴ Actor. If you're not gifted with musical ability but still want to perform in front of people, consider acting.

## *How You Can Move Up*

✴ Get an agent. Agents can help you find jobs and even recording contracts.

✴ Get a regular gig. "House" bands and regular members of touring companies have more steady employment than most musicians.

✴ Become a choreographer or teacher. Dancing is very hard on your body. Many older dancers become choreographers or dance teachers.

✴ Become a superstar. The more people who know your music, the more attention you will gain—perhaps leading to recording contracts and touring!

### *Web Sites to Surf*

**The American Federation of Musicians.** Union offering many benefits, including gig referrals.   http://www.afm.org/public/home/index.php

**DanceUSA.** Community resource for the dance community. http://www.danceusa.org/

**MySpace.** A terrific site for promoting your music. http://www.myspace.com

Help to sell products and services

# Model, Product Demonstrator

Meet exciting people and travel to interesting places

Experience the glamour of professional modeling

# Model, Product Demonstrator

By making a product seem attractive, useful, fun, or high-class, a model or product demonstrator can influence people's buying decisions. A product demonstrator may also provide useful information on how a particular product works and why it is the best on the market for a certain purpose. Moreover, the modeling industry has also become an end to itself in recent years, with "supermodels" becoming celebrities in their own rights. Most models and product demonstrators, however, aren't rich and famous. They work at trade shows, retail stores, and shopping malls around the nation. According to the U.S. Department of Labor, models and product demonstrators hold about 120,000 jobs in the United States. Of these, only about 2,200 are models.

## Is This Job for You?

To find out if being a model or product demonstrator is right for you, read each of the following questions and answer "Yes" or "No."

| | | | |
|---|---|---|---|
| Yes | No | **1.** | Do you enjoy working with people? |
| Yes | No | **2.** | Do you like being the center of attention? |
| Yes | No | **3.** | Are you a good communicator? |
| Yes | No | **4.** | Are you comfortable with yourself? |
| Yes | No | **5.** | Do people consider you attractive and fun to be with? |
| Yes | No | **6.** | Can you follow directions? |
| Yes | No | **7.** | Do you have a strong work ethic? |
| Yes | No | **8.** | Are you not discouraged by rejection? |
| Yes | No | **9.** | Do you know how to separate business and pleasure? |
| Yes | No | **10.** | Do you always plan ahead? |

If you answered "Yes" to most of these questions, you might want to consider a career as a model or product demonstrator. To find out more about these jobs, read on.

## *Let's Talk Money*

The Canadian supermodel Linda Evangelista once infamously said, "I don't get out of bed for less than $10,000," but most models and product demonstrators make far less. According to the U.S. Department of Labor, the median income for product demonstrators is $9.95 per hour, but can vary between $7.25 and $20.08. Models make a median of $10.50, but can earn between $7.16 and $17.17. Very well-paid models can make $30,000–$50,000 per day, but this is rare. One fringe benefit is samples of the product or clothing you are demonstrating or modeling.

## *What You'll Do*

Product demonstrators work in shopping malls, outdoor fairs, supermarkets, lecture halls, or even on television—anywhere there is a product to be sold. They must catch the attention of potential consumers, show them the product, and persuade them to buy it. Some try to address individuals or small crowds, some speak to large audiences, and some work in specialized events such as trade shows. For instance, the video game industry's annual Electronic Entertainment Expo, held every May in Los Angeles, is well known for its many product demonstrators, who often dress in costumes related to the video games they are promoting. Product demonstrators may show how a product works or even give a presentation about its various features or benefits, sometimes using audio-visual materials. Some engage in what is known as *guerilla marketing*, in which they use unconventional or creative means to get people to buy products ranging from toasters to cars.

Models tend to work either live (such as *runway models* during fashion shows) or with photographers. They promote clothes, perfumes, beauty products, accessories, cars, or anything else that people want to sell. There are two basic types of modeling: *high-fashion* and *commercial*. High-fashion models work with high-fashion designers and in fashion magazines such as *Vogue* and *Elle*. (Models who appear in print are often referred to as *editorial models*.) Like actors, they must be able to demonstrate a variety of emotions and moods. You don't have to be stick-thin to be a model! Though high-fashion

## Let's Talk Trends

According to the Department of Labor, the number of models and product demonstrators will grow about as fast as average through 2014. While the field of modeling is highly competitive, as the economy continues to grow, there will be a need for good, skilled product demonstrators willing to work on short notice.

models must have striking features and a very angular, thin build, *commercial* modeling is open to a wider range of body types. Commercial models sell swimsuits, cosmetics, catalog clothing, and other products outside the world of high fashion. There are also other sorts of modeling. For instance, *fitness* models are chosen because they are in excellent shape and have attractive physiques.

## Where You'll Work

More than half model and product demonstrator jobs are short-term freelance positions. Other positions last less than six months. About one-quarter have variable work schedules. Often models or product demonstrators are hired just for one photo shoot or event. Most models and product demonstrators must find outside work in order to make ends meet.

Models may work in any environment imaginable, from clean, well-lit studios and fashion houses to location shoots in hot, steamy jungles or the frozen Vermont countryside in winter. They may be asked to model for photographers or for live audiences, such as on a runway show. Product demonstrators may work anywhere products are shown or sold, from convention centers to markets to malls to nightclubs. Some appear in commercials or "infomercials" for television. Trade shows, such as boat shows or auto shows, are also places where product demonstrators might be found. Usually, employers will pay for the cost of traveling to locations. While most models are based in New York, Los Angeles, London, Paris, or Milan, product demonstrators can be found around the country. Almost all fashion models are based out of New York, since this is where their agencies are located.

Hours vary widely. A job may involve just a few hours at a shopping center, or it may be a 14-hour marathon photo shoot. Thought the work can be tiring, it is not usually strenuous or dangerous.

# The Inside Scoop: Q&A

**Whitney Avalon**
**Model/product demonstrator**
**Needham, Massachusetts**

**Q:** *How did you get your job?*

**A:** Working in promotions and demonstrations, whether at trade shows or in guerilla marketing campaigns on the street, requires that you have signed up with the agencies and casting contacts in your area. No degree is required, just a clear head shot and body shot that shows what you look like right *now*, a positive attitude and the ability to engage strangers in upbeat conversation, and an ability to arrive on time and ready to work.

**Q:** *What do you like best about your job?*

**A:** It's so wonderful to be able to interact with all different types of people in the course of a day, particularly if you're talking about a product that you truly support or offering a deal that you truly believe people should take advantage of. Generally, not having to sit behind a desk all day is a major perk.

**Q:** *What's the most challenging part of your job?*

**A:** Sometimes it's difficult to be on your feet all day and remain up-beat and attentive, but this is precisely what the job requires. Late-night partying prior to a 10-hour workday in the blinding sun is not a good idea.

**Q:** *What are the keys to success as a model or product demonstrator?*

**A:** The key to success (in addition to a base of some amount of inher-ent talent, attractiveness, and dedication) is continually working to the best of your ability. Be early for every call. Be dressed in the clothes they requested, ironed and neat. Always have a smile on your face. Do not take breaks or answer phone calls until a man-ager tells you to do so. Keep the client's tagline or product infor-mation in mind during every conversation. Work hard, and you'll continue to work!

# Your Typical Day

Here are the highlights of a typical day for a model.

✔ **Behind the scenes.** You're due on the set hours before the shoot even begins. An army of hair stylists and makeup artists makes sure your hair and face are perfect for the camera.

✔ **Hold that pose.** Modeling is more than just looking pretty! You need to follow the photographer's directions, show emotions, and capture just the right "look." In many ways, modeling is like acting.

✔ **Take a break.** The upside of working in cities such as New York is the exciting nightlife. After the shoot, you head off to the latest club, where you're the center of attention.

# Who You'll Work For

⭐ Retail companies
⭐ Manufacturers
⭐ Magazines
⭐ Clothing designers

# What You Can Do Now

⭐ Get professionally done head shots.
⭐ Take care of yourself. Eat right, exercise, and stay in shape.
⭐ Pay attention in school. Modeling is only a full-time job for a lucky few, and you will need something to fall back on.

# What Training You'll Need

There are no schools for product demonstrators. Most learn on the job, usually receiving instructions from the marketing team of the company they are working for. While there are schools for models, they can cost a lot of money and opinions are divided on how useful they are. In fact, most modeling agencies prefer models who haven't been to these schools.

While, there is little formal training in the world of modeling and product demonstrating, getting a job can be an art in itself. See "How to Find a Job," below, for more details. Meanwhile, pay attention to your hair, clothes, and makeup. Most importantly, eat right, exercise, and stay in shape.

## How to Talk Like a Pro

Here are a few words you'll hear as a model or product demonstrator:

- ✴ **Guerilla marketing** A low-budget campaign that seeks to subtly influence people's buying choices, such as spray-painting logos for a new movie on a sidewalk or an attractive couple not-so-quietly ordering a certain drink in a nightclub.
- ✴ **Agency** Companies who employ models generally book them through agencies. Being signed to an agency is therefore essential for working as a model.
- ✴ **Go-see** A casting call for modeling. Generally, you will be sent to go-sees by your agency.

## How to Find a Job

The first and most important thing in finding a job as a model or product demonstrator is to sign with an agency. The agency is a company that acts as a middleman between clients and models. It sets you up with jobs, collects your fees, and ensures that you are paid. There are agencies throughout the country handling various sorts of modeling and product demonstration work. However, the largest and most important are in New York and, to a lesser extent, Los Angeles.

In order to sign with an agency, you will need several things. The first is a portfolio of photos of you showing various "looks." These must be professionally done, and represent a considerable investment. You will also need *comp cards*, which are photos of you sent out to potential clients. A cell phone is also essential, since you might be called for a *go-see,* or interview with a potential client. Having the proper sorts of clothes and the skill to properly do your hair and makeup for the go-see are essential. Bringing your portfolio and studying what sort of "look" or emotion the client expects will help you land the job. Be sure to get all possible information from your agent.

Other things necessary to landing jobs, such as self-presentation and networking skills, are more intangible. Being a people person is essential, for instance, for getting your name and picture in agencies' catalogs. One of the most important things about modeling, however, is entirely out of your control. This is your body type and build. While there are all sorts of modeling jobs open to people of all body types, fashion models tend to be naturally tall and thin. Be realistic when choosing the niche that's right for you.

## Secrets *for Success*

See the suggestions below and turn to the appendix for advice on résumés and interviews.

- ✦ The single most important factor in modeling success is attitude. Be sure to have the right one!
- ✦ Be attentive on the job site so you're always ready when needed. A reputation for being professional can be an asset in itself.
- ✦ Product demonstrators should have fallback, which may include some of the occupations listed below in "Some Other Jobs to Think About."

## Reality *Check*

There are very, very few successful professional models, and product demonstrators' work is intermittent. Be sure to have a fallback job.

## Some *Other Jobs to Think About*

- ✦ Real estate sales. Like models and product demonstrators, real estate sales rely a lot on personal charisma.
- ✦ Insurance sales. If you can convince people to buy various sorts of products, why not get a more stable job selling insurance?
- ✦ Actor. Actors, like models, spend a lot of time in front of the camera, but the range of personalities and body types is much wider.

## How *You Can Move Up*

- ✦ Go into marketing. If you are good at product demonstrating, why not look for work in a marketing department? You could be your company's face at trade shows and promotions.
- ✦ Open an agency. Successful models with contacts and business sense can open their own modeling agency.
- ✦ Become a superstar. Top models can make very good salaries. Of course, very, very few models are "super."

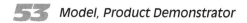 

## Web Sites to Surf

**New Models.** An introduction to the industry for new models.
http://www.newmodels.com/

**Modeling Advice.** Words of wisdom for anyone trying to get into the business.
http://www.modelingadvice.com

*Work with high technology*

# AutoCAD Technician, Graphic Production Technician, Digital Imaging Technician

*Enter an exciting and fast-growing field*

*Learn the latest computer technology*

*Great Careers*

# AutoCAD Technician, Graphic Production Technician, Digital Imaging Technician

Computers and digital imaging have opened up many opportunities for people with visually oriented skills. Today everything from planning office buildings to creating books and magazines to printing vacation photographs is handled by computer. Chief among them is a drafting program called AutoCAD (for "Computer Assisted Design"), which is published by Autodesk. AutoCAD technicians use their software to design and lay out objects in three-dimensional space. Other kinds of software are used to produce everything from postage stamps to books to large highway billboards, or to make digital pictures of anything from the human body to evidence at a crime scene. This information may be used by doctors, insurance companies, law enforcement, or anyone else who has to produce or store data.

## Is This Job for You?

To find out if being an AutoCAD technician, graphic production technician, or digital imaging technician is right for you, read each of the following questions and answer "Yes" or "No."

Yes  No  **1.** Are you good with computers?

Yes  No  **2.** Do you have a keen sense of color and design?

Yes  No  **3.** Do you know how to follow directions?

Yes  No  **4.** Can you manage your time wisely?

Yes  No  **5.** Do you like working as part of a team?

Yes  No  **6.** Do you plan your work carefully?

Yes  No  **7.** Are you methodical and patient in your work?

Yes  No  **8.** Do you have a good sense of space?

Yes  No  **9.** Do you enjoy creative work?

Yes  No  **10.** Can you manage many tasks simultaneously?

If you answered "Yes" to most of these questions, you might want to consider a career as an AutoCAD technician, graphic production technician, or digital imaging technician. To find out more about these jobs, read on.

## *Let's Talk Money*

The average annual income for AutoCAD technicians, graphic production technicians, and digital imaging technicians is about $43,000, according to 2006 statistics from the U.S. Bureau of Labor Statistics. Earnings for the lowest 10 percent of workers—generally those just entering the field—are about $28,000 a year.

## *Who You'll Work For*

✳ Architecture and interior design firms
✳ Universities and scientific firms
✳ Manufacturers
✳ Publishers
✳ Software companies

## *What You'll Do*

AutoCAD technicians use Autodesk's AutoCAD program to produce three-dimensional representations of building interiors, furniture, landscapes, mechanical parts, or other objects. AutoCAD uses simple objects, such as lines, circles, and arcs, to build more complex pictures of proposed projects. These help designers and engineers visualize how a project will work in real space.

Graphic production technician is a career choice that includes a wide range of job descriptions. A graphic production technician may do anything from making and printing signs and advertisements to designing complex visual animations for a video game or training program. These may be designed by the technician herself or by a professional graphic designer. Some of the software used includes Adobe's Illustrator and Photoshop, which are graphics software, and Quark, Inc.'s QuarkXPress, a text layout and design program. The graphic production technicians may operate complicated printers and other machinery.

Digital imaging technicians produce digital pictures, or translate existing pictures into a digital format. These images can be two-dimensional, such as photographs, or three-dimensional, such as images of the human body. Technicians may operate scanners, cameras, three-dimensional imagers, or other complicated equipment. The work can be quite tedious and painstaking, but digital imaging technicians often get to work with the latest scanners, cameras, and other equipment.

# Where You'll Work

Most AutoCAD technicians, graphic production technicians, and digital imaging technicians work in comfortable, well-lit, climate-controlled offices. The offices tend to be a little chilly, since computer equipment requires air-conditioning to keep from overheating. The job tends to involve sitting at a desk, with little moving about. However, AutoCAD technicians, graphic production technicians, and digital imaging technicians, like all workers who use computers for long periods of time, may risk eyestrain, back problems, and joint problems such as carpal tunnel syndrome. They usually work 40-hour weeks, but may need to put in overtime on projects with impending deadlines.

# Your Typical Day

Here are the highlights of a typical day for an AutoCAD technician.

✔ **Get the plan.** Your architecture firm has been hired to redesign the interior of a country club. Today you'll need to input the architect's plans into AutoCAD to see how the designs translate from 2-D to 3-D.

✔ **Meet with the client.** The architect presents your renderings to the client that very afternoon. They are impressed with the plans, but offer some suggestions.

✔ **Burn the midnight oil.** Long after everyone else has left for the night, you're still hard at work, correcting the plans to correspond to the client's wishes.

## Let's Talk Trends

The U.S. Department of Labor does not maintain statistics on AutoCAD technicians, graphic production technicians, or digital imaging technicians. However, to judge from similar occupations, the demand for these workers should increase about as fast as average as industry expands and as new applications for these technologies are implemented.

## *What* You Can Do Now

✴ Learn all you can about AutoCAD and digital imaging software.

✴ Pay attention in school. Mathematics and physics are especially important, and English classes will help you to fluently communicate your designs and ideas.

✴ Potential employers will want to know that you are proficient in the software. Develop a portfolio of designs and other work to show them.

## *What* Training You'll Need

Because there are many types of jobs for AutoCAD technicians, graphic production technicians, and digital imaging technicians, there are many ways to approach this work. Most importantly, you will need to be familiar with the relevant software and hardware. This usually includes Macintosh computers and programs such as Adobe's Photoshop and, of course, Autodesk's AutoCAD. Sometimes you can teach yourself how to use these tools of the trade. It is also possible to take courses at a community college or trade school. Some training may be available on the job. Because many of the software programs and much of the equipment is expensive, it is hard for private individuals or even high schools to acquire it.

Many jobs in graphic design require a college education. However, it's also possible to work your way up from the bottom. If you are skilled at what you do, the sky's the limit.

## *How* to Talk Like a Pro

Here are a few words you'll hear as an AutoCAD technician, graphic production technician, or digital imaging technician:

✴ **AutoCAD** Autodesk's commonly used two- and three-dimensional design program.

✴ **Photoshop** Published by Adobe Systems, this is the industry standard photo-manipulation software. "Photoshop" is also commonly used as a verb for manipulating a picture.

✴ **QuarkXPress** Published by the Quark, Inc., QuarkXPress is a powerful program that enables a user to design and lay out a publication.

# The Inside Scoop: Q&A

**Troy Thompson**
**AutoCAD technician**
**New York, New York**

**Q:** *How did you get your job?*

**A:** It was all about timing. I was looking for a job at the time and walked by this really beautiful furniture showroom in Manhattan. I just randomly asked one of the salespeople if there were any design positions available. They said their AutoCAD technician had just left and they were looking for another, so I sent them my résumé and, after three interviews, I scored the job as an interior designer/AutoCAD tech.

**Q:** *What do you like best about your job?*

**A:** Well I love using AutoCAD, and I get to use it a lot each day working on fun projects of all kinds and sizes, which has helped me improve my CAD skills tremendously.

**Q:** *What's the most challenging part of your job?*

**A:** Since it is a furniture showroom, you have to constantly be on your toes and produce floor plans and other drawings quickly and accurately for clients who are constantly coming in, whether by appointment or not. I make all the AutoCAD drawings in the showroom for six salespeople with dozens and dozens of regular and new clients. I also have other responsibilities in the office, so I'm multitasking all day long.

**Q:** *What are the keys to success as an AutoCAD technician?*

**A:** I'd say, like for any job, you have to have good time-management skills, patience, a good attitude, and the ability to learn quickly and the want to learn more. I think most importantly, you can't take the job too seriously. It's just a job—it shouldn't run your life. There has to be a balance.

# How to Find a Job

Openings for AutoCAD technicians, graphic production technicians, and digital imaging technicians are often posted online or published in newspapers. Most are with large companies. Also look at online message boards such as Craigslist (http://www.craigslist.org). You may also want to send your résumé to architecture firms, print shops, and other businesses if they have any openings. While workers such as these are especially in demand in cities with large publishing industries and high-tech companies, there are opportunities all over the country. Make sure your résumé includes all the computer-related jobs that you have had. If you are looking for experience, consider an unpaid internship or even volunteering for a church or community organization. Being able to show your skill with the requisite software is critical in securing employment.

# Secrets for Success

See the suggestions below and turn to the appendix for advice on résumés and interviews.

- ✦ Keep abreast of the latest technical developments. The technology used in these jobs often changes rapidly. One way to do this is by reading trade magazines and specialist Web sites.
- ✦ Develop your sense of design. Also, it's never too early to learn how to use the required software.

# Reality Check

Many AutoCAD technicians, graphic production technicians, and digital imaging technicians have college degrees. Though work experience counts for much in this field, be aware that you will be competing with college graduates for jobs.

# Some Other Jobs to Think About

- ✦ Photographer. Photographers must also have a keen aesthetic sense, but the work is much less technical.
- ✦ Prepress technician. Prepress technicians work in the same industries and do similar digital imaging work.
- ✦ Desktop publisher. Design and lay out printed materials.

# *How You Can Move Up*

✯ Improve your software skills. The more you learn, the more valuable you are to your employer.

✯ Go back to school. Education often helps workers land more responsible and lucrative jobs.

✯ Start your own business. Once you've saved up some cash, why not start your own printing and duplication company?

## *Web Sites to Surf*

**Digital Imaging Technician.** Advice from skillset.org.
http://www.skillset.org/photo/careers/labs/article_3284_1.asp

**Autodesk.** Publishers of AutoCAD.   http://www.autodesk.com

Be part of a team

# Computer
# Help-Desk
# Specialist

Work in the fast-paced world
of computers

Be a problem solver

# *Computer Help-Desk Specialist*

The call comes in from a panicked office worker: She has to make a presentation in half an hour and she just lost the file she was working on. Is there anything you can do? Fortunately, you are able to diagnose the problem and help her recover her work in the nick of time—just another day in the life of a computer help-desk specialist. If you have a knack for technology, good people skills, and a talent for solving problems, this may be the career for you. With companies small and large relying more and more on computers, computer help-desk specialists are critical to the running of modern businesses. Today there are more than 518,000 computer help-desk specialists working everywhere in America, from high-powered law firms in the office towers of Manhattan to call centers maintained by software companies in rural areas.

## *Is This Job for You?*

To find out if being a computer help-desk specialist is right for you, read each of the following questions and answer "Yes" or "No."

| | | | |
|---|---|---|---|
| *Yes* | *No* | **1.** | Are you a good problem solver? |
| *Yes* | *No* | **2.** | Do you stay calm in high-stress situations? |
| *Yes* | *No* | **3.** | Do people often ask you for help with their computers? |
| *Yes* | *No* | **4.** | Are you patient? |
| *Yes* | *No* | **5.** | Do you have good written and spoken communications skills? |
| *Yes* | *No* | **6.** | Do you like to work indoors in an office environment? |
| *Yes* | *No* | **7.** | Are you good at both giving and following directions? |
| *Yes* | *No* | **8.** | Can you work as part of a team? |
| *Yes* | *No* | **9.** | Are you polite and respectful? |
| *Yes* | *No* | **10.** | Do you like helping people? |

If you answered "Yes" to most of these questions, you might want to consider a career as a computer help-desk specialist. To find out more about this job, read on.

# *What You'll Do*

Computer help-desk specialists generally deal with three types of computer problems: hardware, software, or systems such as computer networks that enable computers to talk to one another. Some computer help-desk specialists deal with all three types of issues, while others focus on a single issue, such as supporting a specific software program or hardware component.

Computer help-desk specialists receive communications from users by e-mail or by phone. Often the customers are anxious or upset. A lot of money—or even their jobs—might be riding on the data in their computers. Other times, the people you are helping have just bought your company's hardware or software product and think that it isn't working properly. Sometimes customers simply don't know how to use their computers properly.

Your job is to diagnose and fix their problems, if possible. If the problem is too complicated, or if you cannot understand what has gone wrong, you may have to refer the user to a specialist with more experience. You will then record the problem and give the user a ticket number. The problem will then be placed in a queue, or list, to be fixed by a second-level member of the support team. These help-desk tracking systems make it easier to manage problems and see what the most common problems are. The tracking system can also help to control workers' time. In such systems, a help-desk specialist may be scheduled to spend a certain amount of time out of every workday tracking problems and a certain amount of time fixing them. Computer and software companies value computer help-desk specialists. Since they are the first to receive customers' complaints about hardware and software, they can provide valuable information on how to improve a product. They can also suggest ways in which products can be made easier to use, and give feedback on what most confuses customers.

## *Let's Talk Money*

According to the U.S. Department of Labor, the median income for computer help-desk specialists is $40,430 but can range between $24,190 and $69,110. Those working for computer software publishers assisting customers tend to make the most, and those working in schools and universities the least.

## *Let's Talk Trends*

Because of the ever-increasing importance of computers in our lives, the number of computer help-desk specialists will grow faster than average through 2014 according to the U.S. Department of Labor. However, "offshoring," or moving call centers to foreign countries where people speak English but wages are much lower, may mean fewer jobs in the United States and Canada.

# *Who* **You'll Work For**

* Software publishers
* Private businesses of all kinds
* Religious and not-for-profit foundations
* Government agencies
* Public and private schools, kindergarten through 12th grade
* Colleges and universities

# *Where* **You'll Work**

Computer help-desk specialists usually work in comfortable, well-lit offices and computer labs. The job sites tend to be a little chilly, since computer equipment requires air-conditioning to keep from overheating. The job tends to involve sitting at a desk, with little moving about. However, some lifting, such as moving and installing new computers, may also be required. Like all workers who use computers for long periods of time, computer help-desk specialists may risk eyestrain, back problems, and joint problems such as carpal tunnel syndrome. Because companies may have customers all over the world in different time zones or employees who work odd hours, computer help-desk specialists may have to work night or weekend shifts.

The size of a computer help-desk specialist's office may have no relation to the size of the organization. A university may have only a few help-desk specialists on call for hundreds or thousands of users, while a relatively small software company may maintain a center staffed with hundreds of employees in order to handle the traffic from thousands or millions of customers. The computer help-desk specialist's day varies widely. You may be more or less busy, waiting for calls or e-mails to come in, or handling one problem after another with very little downtime.

## Your Typical Day

Here are the highlights of a typical day for a computer help-desk specialist at a large company.

✓ **Field some calls.** The day starts getting busy around 9:30 or 10 a.m., when users begin starting up their computers and running into trouble with their work. Some calls will be serious, such as hard-disk crashes that ruin hours of hard work. Some will seem silly, such as the boss who can't read his e-mail since his secretary, who usually prints it out for him, is on vacation. Other things will be routine administrative tasks, such as setting up usernames and passwords for new employees.

✓ **Handle an emergency.** Suddenly, the call board lights up. The server on which the company's employees save their work has crashed. Dozens of users can't get to their important documents. While the network team tries to get it running again, you spend your time on the phone reassuring anxious employees.

✓ **Pull some overtime.** The network team gets the server up and running again, but because of the disruption to the workday you need to stay late. In this case, you spend an extra hour answering users' e-mails from the previous day that you couldn't get to because of the network outage.

## What You Can Do Now

✴ Learn as much as you can. Potential employers will want to know that you know your way around computers.

✴ Practice your written and oral communications skills. A computer help-desk specialist must be polite, professional, and articulate.

✴ See if you can enroll in a training course to obtain certification in specialized software or hardware.

✴ While using your computer, practice describing your actions with words.

# The Inside Scoop: Q&A

**Peter Zillmann**
**Computer help-desk specialist**
**Kalamazoo, Michigan**

**Q:** *How did you get your job?*

**A:** It began as a work/study job. Later I got a call from my former supervisor asking me to fill a temporary position while they completed a job search. When the search was up they asked me if I'd stay on in another position doing hardware, software, printer, network, phone, Web, and e-mail tech support over the phone. I accepted!

**Q:** *What do you like best about your job?*

**A:** Getting to work with and provide help to a wide variety of people.

**Q:** *What's the most challenging part of your job?*

**A:** Learning to manage my reactions to customers' frequently emotional calls. People generally don't call the help desk to say they're happy and that everything is working perfectly for them.

**Q:** *What are the keys to success as a computer help-desk specialist?*

**A:** Remember the Golden Rule. Wonderful people sometimes make stupid mistakes, but they still deserve to be treated like wonderful people. Don't let customers' frustration bring you down. Re-focus yourself before each call and give each caller the benefit of your best effort. You don't have to be cheerful every minute of every day, but you'll go further if people think you are.

## How to Talk Like a Pro

Here are a few words you'll hear as a computer help-desk specialist:

✴ **Server** A central computer that provides services to other computers. It can also act as storage space for data.

✴ **Network** Many computers linked together by servers. Networks can make it easier to share and store data but can create a lot of trouble when they break.

★ **LBT** The "Local Bug Tracker." This is the "queue" into which users' errors are entered and trends recorded. LBTs are very important for tracking problems until they are resolved.

# What Training You'll Need

Though a college degree is not always necessary to work at a help desk, you will likely be competing for jobs with people who have had some college experience. Any advantage you can get, such as a practical familiarity with computers, will help you to get ahead. Since computer systems can be slightly different, computer help-desk specialists will usually also be trained by the companies that employ them. This will usually include familiarization with the various computer programs used by the help desk and the process by which problems are resolved. Later you might be taught how to fix certain malfunctions, such as server crashes. Computer help-desk specialists enjoy great upward mobility and are promoted based on their success at helping customers. As computer help-desk specialists move up in the ranks, they are given more responsibilities, including performing second-level support. Learning how to perform these tasks is often accomplished more by experience than by formal training. At the top levels, they may help guide a company's overall use of computer technology. If further training is required, such as learning how to fix or run certain software, your company may pay for you to take a certification exam.

# How to Find a Job

Companies often place help-wanted ads in newspapers or online message boards such as Craigslist (http://www.craigslist.org). Also consider asking friends and relatives who work in technical support. They may be aware of entry-level openings at their companies or one with which they work. Computer help-desk specialists are in great demand in all sorts of industries, from agribusiness to zoological parks. While computer help-desk specialists are in demand in cities with large high-tech companies such as New York, Portland (home of Amazon.com), and Seattle (home of Microsoft), modern telecommunications mean that call centers also can be located in rural areas. Show your work ethic, communications skills, and level-headed but friendly personality both in your interview and by asking adults who write character references and letters of recommendation for you to emphasize these qualities. Make sure your résumé includes all the computer-related jobs that you have had and all the computer skills you possess. If you are looking for experience, consider an unpaid internship or even volunteering as a moderator on an Internet message board.

## Secrets for Success

See the suggestions below and turn to the appendix for advice on résumés and interviews.

* Be polite and calm. Resist the urge to make fun of users. Many older people see computers as new and scary, and may be afraid of breaking them.
* Get your certification as soon as possible. It's your ticket to moving up.

## Reality Check

Many call centers are dead-end jobs, with little opportunity to move up. Furthermore, screening the same call over and over again can be very tedious. Finally, many users can be rude or downright hostile.

## Some Other Jobs to Think About

* Computer programmer. Many computer programmers are self-taught. If you are a skilled programmer, you can get a well-paying job making programs or games. If you are right for help desk work, you may be a few courses and an interview away from being a programmer.
* Network administrator. Computer network administrators are in charge of building and maintaining companies' computer networks. Though this job often requires advanced certification, such certification may only require some light coursework.
* Quality-assurance specialist. If you don't like dealing with people, but do like tinkering with computers, you might like work as a quality-assurance (QA) specialist. QA is the department in charge of making sure software works as advertised.

# *How You Can Move Up*

✶ Get certified. Some companies, such as Microsoft, have special training courses that teach people how to fix their products. By earning your certification, you can move up to a better-paying job as a network administrator

✶ Keep learning. Did you know many two- and four-year colleges give credit for work experience? You may find your local institution has favorable financial aid policies for working students. Many employers like to see a two- or four-year degree for higher level employees, or even that you're working toward one. If you are working for a college or university, you can usually get free or reduced-cost tuition while you work.

✶ Be persistent. The help desk is usually the first step toward becoming a computer support specialist. Because the computer industry is changing so rapidly, formal training is of limited use. Many computer help-desk specialists learn enough "on the job" to move up.

## Web Sites to Surf

**Help Desk Management Community Portal.** Learn what a help desk is, what it does, and make contact with industry professionals.
http://www.helpdesking.com

**Help Desk Journal.** "Tips and Techniques for Help Desk Excellence." This site will help you learn all about the world of help-desk support.
http://helpdesk.wyopub.com

Exercise your creativity

# Webpage Designer

Work in an exciting hi-tech field

Use sophisticated software

# Webpage Designer

Can anyone imagine life without the Internet? Beginning as a government project in the late 1960s, the Internet grew to enormous size in the mid-1990s after the invention of the World Wide Web. The Web lets us view text, pictures, sound, movies, and animation in an easy, user-friendly way. Finding driving directions, shopping for clothes, and looking up information are now only a few mouse clicks away. The people who make the magic happen are Webpage designers. Webpage designers write the computer code, design the graphics, and maintain the behind-the-scenes technology that keeps Web sites running. While not as fluent in computer code as the programmers who handle the "back end," they work with clients to find out what they want and create sites that elegantly express what the clients have to say.

## Is This Job for You?

To find out if being a Webpage designer is right for you, read each of the following questions and answer "Yes" or "No."

Yes No **1.** Are you good with computers?

Yes No **2.** Are you familiar with the latest technology?

Yes No **3.** Do you have a good sense of color and design?

Yes No **4.** Do you keep at a problem until you solve it?

Yes No **5.** Do you have a good work ethic?

Yes No **6.** Do you listen carefully to others?

Yes No **7.** Do you enjoy learning?

Yes No **8.** Do you not mind working long hours?

Yes No **9.** Are you always curious?

Yes No **10.** Do you like to know what makes things work?

If you answered "Yes" to most of these questions, then you might be cut out for a career as a Webpage designer. To find out more about this job, read on.

## What You'll Do

A Web site can be small and contain only a few pages of text, or be enormous and have sophisticated functions such as message boards, e-commerce capability, and multimedia downloads. No matter what

## Let's Talk Money

The annual income range for Webpage designers begins at about $52,000, and those working in entry-level positions of computer support earn about $40,000 a year on average, according to 2006 figures from the U.S. Bureau of Labor Statistics. Salaries generally track with education and experience, but many in the field are self-taught or have learned their skills while working.

type of Web site it is, though, the "guts" of the World Wide Web is HTML, or *hypertext markup language*. HTML is a code that tells a Web browser how to display images and text on the screen. At the most basic level, a Web site is a number of HTML files linked together. The Webpage designer's job fundamentally consists of writing these files.

However, creating a Web site requires more than just writing HTML. A good Webpage designer knows how to do many other tasks. These include registering a domain name (the address that appears in the navigation toolbar), finding a *host*, or online storage space, to *serve* the Webpages to users who request them. To *serve* a file is to provide it to other computers that request them. A Webpage designer will also know how to configure the server's setup and upload the Web site.

Some Webpage designers use software such as Microsoft's Frontpage and Adobe's Dreamweaver to make Webpages. These *WYSIWYG* (for "what you see if what you get") programs make it easier to see what the finished Webpage will look like. The most successful Webpage designers know how to do far more than this, though. For instance, some know how to craft *PHP* (Personal Home Page tools) code to create dynamic Web sites that can quickly upload and change their content. Others are adept at creating applications, such as online shopping carts, in programming languages such as Sun Microsystem's Java, or creating animations in Adobe's Flash. The more you know how to do, the better your chances of succeeding as a Webpage designer.

## *Who* You'll Work For

✯ All types of businesses
✯ Private individuals
✯ Self

## Let's Talk Trends

Though the U.S. Department of Labor does not keep exact statistics, the number of Webpage designers will probably grow at about an average rate through 2014. Though programmer jobs in general are expected to grow more slowly than average, in part due to automation and offshoring (that is, moving jobs to countries where labor is cheaper), Webpage design must be done by hand and by people who know the client's needs. Clients also like to meet in person with the people, such as Webpage designers, who present their images to the public.

# Where You'll Work

Webpage designers may be self-employed or work for someone else. Those who work for companies generally work in climate-controlled offices—in fact, job sites tend to be a little chilly, since computer equipment has to be kept from overheating. Webpage designing is not a very active occupation, and involves sitting in front of a computer for long stretches of time. This does not mean the job is not without its risks, though: Like all workers who use computers for long periods of time, Webpage designers often complain of eyestrain, back problems, and joint problems such as carpal tunnel syndrome. Of course, if you are a freelance Webpage designer, you can do your work on a laptop while sitting in an air-conditioned café or a park bench on a sunny day.

Hours vary widely. Though a 40-hour week is standard, Webpage designers may work long hours on projects. This is because of the need to meet deadlines, the general culture of the industry, and individual personalities—Webpage designers tend to be perfectionists. Freelancers tend to work irregularly. They may have more work than they can handle one week, and little the next.

# Your Typical Day

Here are the highlights of a typical day for a Webpage designer.

✔ **Meet and greet.** Your company has been hired to do the Web site for a clothing company's new product line. Before beginning the project, though, you have to organize. Some people will handle the graphics, while some will handle the programming.

✔ **Do a mockup.** Back at your desk, you quickly translate some ideas into HTML code. Soon you have a working model of how the site will look.

✔ **Back to the drawing board.** The site is presented to the client later that afternoon, and they offer their critiques. Unfortunately, they want a complete revision. You'll be working on follow-up changes all day tomorrow. This is going to be a long project!

# *The Inside Scoop: Q&A*

**Brent Johnson**
**Webpage designer**
**Berkeley, California**

**Q:** *How did you get your job?*

**A:** I created a humor site with friends who wanted an unfiltered voice on the Web. It wasn't really sophisticated or pretty, or for that matter really funny, but it did help me establish credentials to getting my current job.

**Q:** *What do you like best about your job?*

**A:** I just like making Web sites. You have an idea, develop your content, design a Web site to present it, and there it is! You can instantly get your ideas in people's faces. Especially with my own site, I liked control, being "the decider" of what appears.

**Q:** *What's the most challenging part of your job?*

**A:** The challenge is what makes it rewarding, I guess. I like creating the content, but maintaining and updating a Web site can be rather time-consuming and eventually tedious. That's why I stopped updating my original site. It's a lot easier if you're getting paid for it!

**Q:** *What are the keys to success as a Webpage designer?*

**A:** The key to success is persistence. For about four years we continually updated the site, developed new content, made friends via boards and Web associations, which led to more and more links from quality sites. Basically, we had something going for us, but it took a lot of work for people to know we even existed—but once they did, traffic shot up.

# *What* You Can Do Now

✯ Learn HTML, Flash, PHP, and everything else you need to know for the job.

✯ Create Web sites of your own using these technologies to show prospective clients and employers.

✯ Network with other Web professionals. They can help to get your work seen.

# *What* Training You'll Need

There is no one career path for entering the world of Webpage design. While there are schools, courses, and certificate programs, these are not, strictly speaking, necessary. What is more important is that a designer can do good work, understands the technology, and (in large companies) cooperates with others. To this end, work experience matters more than education. See "How to Find a Job," below, for tips on how to gain experience.

Many programmers and Webpage designers learn the technical aspects on their own. There are books that teach the elements, which many find very useful. There are also online tutorials that you can use. Other aspiring Webpage designers ask questions on Internet message boards, learning from more experienced programmers and designers. One way to start is to simply click on "view" and then "page source" (or just hit "Ctrl" and "U") when viewing a Webpage. This will show you the HTML code for the page. Download it to your own computer, take it, and play with it.

Most important is a good sense of aesthetics and design. Nobody likes a site in garish colors with blinking text and crude graphics (except, perhaps, as a joke). Look at sites you like and try to imitate them. Experiment with different color schemes and layout. Meanwhile, pay attention in computer, math, and art classes, as these will serve you well later.

# *How* to Talk Like a Pro

Here are a few words you'll hear as a Webpage designer:

✯ **WYSIWYG** "What You See is What You Get," the generic name for a program that designs Webpages. You can graphically manipulate the parts of the page, such as text and images, on-screen, and it will automatically generate the code. Unfortunately, the code is not always as "clean" and elegant as a hand-coded Web site.

* **PHP** Personal Home Page tools, a way of creating dynamic and quickly-changing content. A PHP-driven Web site can, for instance, fit articles coded into PHP format into a generic template.
* **Flash** A program published by Adobe that adds animation and interactivity to Web sites.

## How to Find a Job

Perhaps the easiest way to get started in Webpage design is to simply ask someone, "Can I design a Web site for you?" In order to get work, it helps to have a portfolio of sites that you've created. This not only shows your talents, but will help you compete against applicants with more education by showing that you can actually do the job.

If you want to do freelance Webpage design, you can find clients by sending out flyers and letters to local businesses, hanging flyers, and other direct methods. You should also post on online message boards such as Craigslist (http://www.craigslist.org) and, of course, create a Web page of your own for clients to see! If you are good at what you do, then old clients will recommend you to new ones.

In order to find opportunities at already existing businesses, look in the local newspaper, and, especially in online job boards. Also ask people who work in the industry. Very often, they will know if local companies are hiring.

## Secrets for Success

See the suggestions below and turn to the appendix for advice on résumés and interviews.

* Pay attention to a client's wishes—but also know when what they want is impractical or not suited to their needs.
* Keep on top of new technology. The Web is changing every day, and more and more features are being added.

## Reality Check

While Webpage design is interesting and creative work, you will be competing in the job market against people with college degrees. Be sure your work is better than theirs!

## *Some Other Jobs to Think About*

✦ Computer help-desk specialist. If you're good at fixing computer problems, why not do it for a living?

✦ Computer network technician. Set up and repair computer systems.

✦ Graphic production technician. Create graphics without having to learn computer coding.

## *How You Can Move Up*

✦ Learn more. The more you can do, the better your job opportunities.

✦ Start your own business. If you have a lot of clients, why not go into business for yourself?

✦ Become a programmer. Go back to school or get your certification to work on the "back end."

### Web Sites to Surf

**Devlounge.** Useful community Web site for Web developers.
http://www.devlounge.net

**Designertalk.** Another valuable community site.
http://www.designerstalk.com/forums

**Jakob Nielsen.** Site of Web usability guru Jakob Nielsen.
http://www.useit.com

*Enjoy good job stability*

# Computer Network Technician

*Learn to build and maintain computer networks*

*Work with the latest technologies*

# *Computer Network Technician*

With the increasing computerization of the workforce, many specialized and very important jobs have emerged to help organize and maintain companies' computer resources. Computer network technicians build, maintain, and operate networks—systems by which computers share information and access e-mail. Without these computer networks, many companies' ability to do business would grind to a halt. Computer network technicians are most important to businesses that deal in information, such as insurance brokers, software publishers, and stock traders. Since the main qualification for the job is obtaining and maintaining certificates to run a variety of server applications, being a computer network technician is a very lucrative and stable career you can begin without having to go to college. It is also a popular career choice: According to the U.S. Department of Labor, there are about 292,000 computer network technicians working in the United States today.

## *Is This Job for You?*

To find out if being a computer network technician is right for you, read each of the following questions and answer "Yes" or "No."

| | | | |
|---|---|---|---|
| *Yes* | *No* | **1.** | Are you a good problem solver? |
| *Yes* | *No* | **2.** | Are you good with computers? |
| *Yes* | *No* | **3.** | Can you work as part of a team? |
| *Yes* | *No* | **4.** | Are you very patient? |
| *Yes* | *No* | **5.** | Do you have good written and spoken communication skills? |
| *Yes* | *No* | **6.** | Do you like to work indoors in an office environment? |
| *Yes* | *No* | **7.** | Are you good at both giving and following directions? |
| *Yes* | *No* | **8.** | Do you stay calm in high-stress situations? |
| *Yes* | *No* | **9.** | Can you understand and process complex problems? |
| *Yes* | *No* | **10.** | Do you like helping people? |

If you answered "Yes" to most of these questions, you might be right for a career as a computer network technician. To find out more about this job, read on.

## Let's Talk Money

The Department of Labor does not keep statistics on computer network technicians, who may be classified as network administrators or as network system and data communications analysts. The median income for network administrators is $58,190, but can vary between $37,100 and $91,300. According to Robert Half International, starting salaries in 2005 ranged from $26,500 to $53,750 for network support staff. Those with more education tend to be higher earners.

# What You'll Do

Computer network technicians are in charge of building, maintaining, and supporting computer networks—that is, workers' personal computers linked by fiber-optic cables to *servers*. Servers are powerful central computers that store and deliver computer files to users' computers as they are needed. There are several different companies that manufacture servers, all of which program their machines to work slightly differently. A computer network technician may know how to work with one or more of these systems.

A network has capabilities beyond simply serving files, of course. It may be used for telecommunications, such as Voice Over Internet Protocol (VOIP). It is also how a company connects its workers to the Internet. You may be in charge of maintaining security features such as *filters*, which prevent users for accessing certain Web sites, or *firewalls*, which prevent intruders from getting into your company's computers. There are also routine tasks, such as giving new employees access to the network and backing up files.

## Let's Talk Trends

Because of the ever-increasing importance of computers in the economy and companies' interest in securing their networks, the number of computer network technicians will grow much faster than average through 2014. Because computer network technicians must be present on-site, the industry is insulated from "offshoring," or moving call centers to foreign countries where people speak English but wages are much lower.

## *Who You'll Work For*

✴ Software publishers
✴ Private businesses of all kinds
✴ Government agencies
✴ Public and private schools, kindergarten through 12th grade
✴ Colleges and universities

## *Where You'll Work*

Computer network technicians usually work in comfortable, well-lit offices and computer labs. Since computers require air-conditioning to keep them from overheating, offices tend to be a little chilly. Though some physical labor is required, such as lifting, moving, and installing new computers, the computer network technician's job tends to be sedentary. When computer network technicians find themselves gaining weight, many blame their jobs! Also, like all workers who use computers for long stretches of time, computer network technicians are at risk for eyestrain, back problems, and joint problems such as carpel tunnel syndrome. Regular exercise helps to prevent these problems. Because companies may have customers all over the world in different time zones or employees who work odd hours, computer network technicians may have to work night or weekend shifts. They may also need to put in overtime during crises, such as system crashes, or when performing upgrades, since this is usually done during off-hours so as not to interfere with users' work.

The size of a computer network technician's office may have no relation to the size of the organization. A university may only have a few computer network technicians on call for hundreds or thousands of users, while a relatively small software company may maintain a sizable staff. A computer network technician's workload varies widely: One day you may only need to assign a username to a new employee, while the next, the entire system may come crashing down.

## *What You Can Do Now*

✴ Learn everything you can. Potential employers will want to know that you know computer systems.
✴ Enroll in a training course to obtain certification.
✴ If you can, get specialized training in network security. This will add to your attractiveness to an employer.

# The Inside Scoop: Q&A

**Edgar de La Vega**
**Computer network technician**
**New York, New York**

**Q:** *How did you get your job?*

**A:** I was offered a part-time, night-shift position at a hospital from a project manager whom I've worked with in the past. He happens to be the Information Technology Operations Manager at that same facility. I watch the servers to make sure nothing crashes and back up the files.

**Q:** *What do you like best about your job?*

**A:** The night shift is quiet, and since I'm also going to school while I work, I can study during downtime when there aren't any computer users to attend to.

**Q:** *What's the most challenging part of your job?*

**A:** The challenging part is the backing up of various application servers during the night. I like doing that, though.

**Q:** *What are the keys to success as a computer network technician?*

**A:** One must listen and follow up on the requested needs of clients and supervisors. Positive work relationships ought to be cultivated with your peers, thereby solidifying potential work contacts and references for the future. Finally, the value of the suggestions you put forth toward solving a perceived problem displays initiative and flexible thinking.

## Your Typical Day

Here are the highlights of a typical day for a computer network technician working for a large corporation.

✔ **A few administrative tasks.** The day starts with a few normal duties—creating network accounts for new employees, checking to make sure the night shift backed up the servers, and the usual paperwork.

✓ **All of a sudden . . .** The call comes in: One of the servers has gone down. Hundreds of workers can't get to their files. The network technician staff springs into action.

✓ **Problem resolved.** After some diagnostics and searching, you trace the problem to a burned-out motherboard in one of the servers. You quickly swap the broken board for a new one and reboot the system. Once again the day is saved, thanks to the computer network technician. To wind down, you spend a few hours after lunch learning the ins and outs of a new scheduling program management is thinking about deploying company-wide, but which you need to check out first.

## *How to Talk Like a Pro*

Here are a few words you'll hear as a computer network technician:

✯ **Firewall** The security barrier between a company's network and the outside world.

✯ **Server** A central computer that provides services to other computers. They can also act as storage spaces for data.

✯ **Network** Many computers linked together by fiber-optic cables and servers.

## *What Training You'll Need*

Though a college degree is not always necessary to work as a computer network technician, many colleges and technical schools offer courses toward certification as a computer network technician. This usually includes basic electronic theory and instruction toward a certification exam. Computer network technicians are also sometimes trained by the companies that employ them, especially if they begin at the bottom, for instance as a help-desk specialist. Another venue for training is the armed forces. The navy, for instance, makes great use of computer network technicians (where they are known as information systems technicians). Training will usually include familiarization with the various servers, systems, and procedures.

Servers run on several different operating systems. In order to have the best employment opportunities, you must pass a certification exam for a specific operating system, such as Microsoft, Sun,

Cisco, or Red Hat (for Linux). Of these, the best-known is the Microsoft Certified Systems Engineer, or MCSE. The exams cost $125 to $150 to take. Upon passing, students are considered qualified to build and maintain computer systems using that operating system. You can find many self-study books for these exams in libraries, bookstores, and online. There are also courses you can take to prepare for the exam.

## *How to Find a Job*

Because people in the computer network technician field are used to computers and the Internet, companies often place help-wanted ads on Internet job sites or message boards such as Craigslist (http://www.craigslist.org). Another method for finding a job is asking friends and relatives who work in network engineering or technical support. They may be aware of an entry-level opening at their companies or one with which they work. While the best-paid jobs are in large, geographically central, or technology-driven cities such as New York, Toronto, Chicago, and Seattle, computer network technicians are in great demand in all sorts of businesses, especially those that deal with data and information. Make sure that your certifications are up-to-date and that your references and letters of recommendation emphasize your skill with computers. Also make sure your résumé includes all the computer-related jobs that you have had. If you are looking for experience, consider an unpaid internship or even beginning as a computer help-desk specialist. Though your total related experience can help, it is also important that you show a potential employer that you are eager to learn. Think about what would make you right for the job, develop your skills, and be positive.

## *Secrets for Success*

See the suggestions below and turn to the appendix for advice on résumés and interviews.

* Know everything you can about your servers and your jobs. Technology changes quickly and there's no time to stop learning for computer professionals.
* Machines are just an important part of the job. How you deal with people, and how well you understand their needs, will significantly determine your success.

# *Reality* Check

Being a computer network technician can be frustrating. Many people don't understand how networks and systems work—and they expect you to go along with their ill-informed ideas.

# *Some* Other Jobs to Think About

* Computer help-desk specialist. Why not begin in technical support while studying for your certification? Help-desk specialists rarely require special training.
* AutoCAD technician, graphic production technician, digital imaging technician. These computer workers do not need advanced certification—just know-how.
* Computer programmer. Many computer programmers are self-taught. If you are a skilled programmer, you can get a well-paying job making programs or games. If you are qualified to be a network technician, you may also easily be able to become a programmer!

# *How* You Can Move Up

* Get certified. Get that certification! Not only does it mean more money, it means advancement.
* Keep learning. Many employers like to see a two- or four-year degree for higher-level employees, or even that you're working toward one. You may find your local institution has favorable financial aid policies for working students, and that they give credit for work experience. Computer network technicians enjoy great upward mobility and are often promoted based more on their performance in their jobs than their education. At the top levels, computer network technicians may help create an organization's information-technology policies.
* Be persistent. Because the computer industry is changing so rapidly, formal training other than certification classes is of limited use. Many computer help-desk specialists learn enough "on the job" to move up. In time, you may become a supervisor or administrator.

## Web Sites to Surf

**Sun Microsystems.** Sun's page on obtaining certification for the Solaris operating system. http://www.sun.com/training/certification/solaris/index.html

**Microsoft Certified Systems Engineer.** Microsoft's page on becoming a Certified systems engineer. http://www.microsoft.com/learning/mcp/mcse/

*Exercise your creativity*

# Handicrafts-person

*Help to make props for TV and movies*

*Work in an exciting and creative industry*

# Handicraftsperson

Who do you think gets the most work in the TV and motion picture industries? Actors? Directors? No—it's handicraftspersons. The art department, in which handicraftspersons work, is the single largest department on a movie set. It is responsible for creating the "look" of the film and includes such elements as design, construction, props, special effects, costume, and others. Job titles include painters, riggers, sculptors, prop makers, model makers, stagehands, special effects, and may even be considered to include animal handlers and armorers. It is hard to say how many people work as handicraftspersons in the U.S. film industry, but according to the U.S. Department of Labor, 10,000 work in arts and entertainment as set and exhibit designers or as artists and related professionals. Handicraftspersons work in music, theater, and stage productions too. According to the Department of Labor, there are 34,000 designers and artists working in music and related professions.

## Is This Job for You?

To find out if being a handicraftsperson is right for you, read each of the following questions and answer "Yes" or "No."

Yes  No  **1.** Can you move permanently to where a job is?

Yes  No  **2.** Do you mind working long or irregular hours?

Yes  No  **3.** Can you improvise well?

Yes  No  **4.** Are you very organized?

Yes  No  **5.** Are you strong and in good shape?

Yes  No  **6.** Are you very creative?

Yes  No  **7.** Do you work well under pressure?

Yes  No  **8.** Are you willing to start at the bottom?

Yes  No  **9.** Are you a team player?

Yes  No  **10.** Do you have good communications skills?

If you answered "Yes" to most of these questions, you might want to consider a career as a handicraftsperson. To find out more about this job, read on.

# *What You'll Do*

From stagehands to special effects, handicraftspeople fall into many different categories. Most are in the art department, the part of a movie or theater production that is responsible for the overall look and feel. While many of the jobs in the art department, such as production designer, are senior positions that involve researching and planning the overall look of the production, handicraftspersons are critical for realizing this plan.

*Special effects* workers have many specialties. They may operate mechanical dinosaurs or radio-controlled airplanes or be responsible for the gory splatter-factor in a horror movie. *Pyrotechnicians,* a subspecialty of special effects workers, may set up and detonate anything from large explosions to *squibs,* or small explosive charges. Other pyrotechnic devices, such as fireworks, are also their responsibility. Special effects workers also may use computers to fill in other effects after shooting is finished.

As their job description suggests, *prop* and *model makers* make props—anything from a stone axe for a caveman to a corsage for the prom queen to an intergalactic spaceship that will be shot close-up. They may order their own materials, particularly if they are freelancers, or they may leave this to the buyers. They will usually also offer feedback to the design department on how a particular idea is working out.

*Carpenters, painters,* and other skilled trades are also essential to the production of motion pictures and stage shows. They make and decorate sets and some props. How to train to be a carpenter is dealt with more fully in *Great Careers with a High School Diploma: Construction and Trades.*

## *Let's Talk Money*

It is hard to estimate handicraftspersons's earnings, because so much of the work is irregular and because of the wide variety of positions. The median income for all workers in arts and entertainment is $313 per week. Workers with regular jobs, such as with long-running Broadway shows and Hollywood production companies, will tend to be paid according to their specialty, such as carpenters and electricians. Workers who are union members will be paid according to union rates.

## Let's Talk Trends

It is hard to estimate growth in the number of handicraftspersons. There may be less growth, due to many movies now being filmed overseas. There will also be a lot of competition for jobs in this highly desirable and interesting industry.

Other miscellaneous jobs in the art department include *property buyers*, who purchase needed props (or the components for the props), *armorers*, who keep track of all the weapons used on a film and make sure that the actors and crew know how to use them properly, and *animal handlers*, who train everything from rats and roaches to horses and elephants and ensure the safety of their charges.

*Set dressers*, *stagehands*, and other workers who move or operate things instead of making them are dealt with in the chapter of this book on grips, stagehands, and set-up workers.

## *Who* You'll Work For

✴ TV production companies
✴ Movie studios
✴ Local TV stations
✴ Commercial production companies
✴ Theaters and theater companies
✴ Musicians and touring companies

## *Where* You'll Work

Most openings for handicraftspersons are in Los Angeles or New York, since these cities both have large theater scenes and because many movies, television shows, and commercials are shot there. Handicraftspersons generally work indoors in shops and production companies, but for filming on location, they may need to travel to distant parts of the country or the world. However, unlike grips, stagehands, and set-up workers, handicraftspersons do not always need to be on the set, and so are less likely to travel.

Hours in the entertainment industry can be very irregular, with 14- to 18-hour days one month followed by long periods of unemployment. However, handicraftspersons in the motion picture industry tend to work for large craft houses, and so have more regular jobs than many other works. Also, if you are working for certain productions, such as a Broadway show, you might have a fairly regular work schedule.

Generally, the work is not particularly dangerous (with some exceptions, such as working with firearms or high explosives), but it can be stressful to work under pressure. Often you will have to complete one part of a movie's props while another is being shot.

# *Your* Typical Day

Here are the highlights of a typical day for a handicraftsperson working in the film industry.

✓ **Planning stages.** The first step before making anything is to find out what's expected of you. Today, for instance, you meet with the production designer and the director to find out how they want the inside of the spaceship *Lightning Bug* to look for their new film *Lightning Bug II: Cowboys in Space.* By the end of the meeting, you have a list of detailed instructions and sketches.

✓ **Send out the buyer.** You compose a shopping list of what you'll need to construct the set. This is then given to the buyer, whose job it is to find all the various things for the job.

✓ **Make it!** The cockpit of the *Lightning Bug* arrives at your workshop in the form of sheet metal, tubing, piping, and disassembled chairs from an office-supply store. By next week, though, you'll have this looking like a spaceship from the twenty-sixth century.

# *What* You Can Do Now

✗ Work making props and special effects for student productions, independent movies, Web features, and anything else you can find. Do everything you can to gain experience.

✗ Study everything you can about how props and special effects for movies and TV shows are made. There are some trade magazines you can read.

# The Inside Scoop: Q&A

**Melina Hammer**
**Handicraftsperson**
**New York, New York**

**Q:** *How did you get your job?*

**A:** I got my job through a muddy college journey. It turned out I hated my chosen course, and I've been making work in metal ever since. It's more my life pursuit than a job, and each piece is a learning experience. I love the freedom of creating.

**Q:** *What do you like best about your job?*

**A:** Most rewarding is the sense of creating something from nothing—there is an immense feeling of satisfaction at seeing something through, from concept to actual physical object, never mind that it attaches me to the lineage of metalworkers throughout all human history. I also cherish the effect my work has over people: Continuously, the public will stare, or start in on spontaneous conversation at the uniqueness, or otherwise striking quality of my finished products.

**Q:** *What's the most challenging part of your job?*

**A:** Most challenging is making sure there are enough people tapped into my endeavors, so that I can feed myself and pay my bills. There is no clear "road to success" in my chosen field; it is a constant hustle. My lifestyle is not as stable as in other professions; I am continuously seeking new outlets so that my work may be further promoted and found valuable by others, so that they will share in my vision and help me continue making pieces that are compelling and powerful.

**Q:** *What are the keys to success as a handicraftsperson?*

**A:** The keys to success are varied: It helps to be talented and possess a unique vision that shows in the making of each piece. Once original talent is taken care of, having a broad network of supporters or contacts is indispensable. This is a foundation for the promise of a bright future, as these people will be there to bounce ideas off

*(Continued on next page)*

*(continued from previous page)*

of, help spread word about the specialness of your creativity, and serve as first (and repeat) clients for your distinctive, beautiful work. A job under someone experienced—in the same field—can provide valuable information not readily available. It is like an extension of an internship, or apprenticeship. Many gems of knowledge are passed along in this setting, especially if there is a good working relationship.

## *What* Training You'll Need

Some handicraftspersons are self-trained or trained informally on the job. This is definitely an industry where you learn by doing and where experience counts. For this reason, it is best to get as much experience as possible to build up your résumé. Try to join community theater or independent movie productions. Many prop makers began by getting starter jobs at production houses. The most important thing is to have a talent and a passion for what you're doing and not to mind working long hours.

Other handicraftsperson jobs require a lot more training. Working with explosives or firearms, for instance, requires special permits and a lot of training. Many pyrotechnicians and armorers are former military or law-enforcement personnel. Some handicraftspersons also apprentice to more experienced workers. Carpenters often begin as carpenter's helpers and work their way up through experience. They may also attend technical or trade schools.

## *How* to Talk Like a Pro

Here are the sorts of props a handicraftsperson might handle:

- ✴ **Dressing prop** The furniture, carpets, and other decor used to decorate a set.
- ✴ **Hand prop** Any prop held by an actor, such as a laser gun or a riding crop.
- ✴ **Hero prop** A prop that is central to the action in a scene, such as an ancient artifact being grabbed by an intrepid archaeologist.

* **Stunt prop** A prop especially made to make stunts safer, such as a blunt, spring-loaded knife or a bottle made of "sugar glass."
* **Mechanical prop** A prop that moves or lights up.

# How to Find a Job

Production companies who employ handicraftspersons sometimes advertise in newspapers, free weeklies, and trade publications. Look also on Web sites such as Craigslist (http://www.craigslist.org) or Variety.com. Most handicraftspersons belong to unions, such as the International Alliance of Theatrical Stage Employees, Moving Picture Technicians, Artists, and Allied Crafts. These unions can be very helpful for finding jobs for their members. Most maintain some sort of job board or employment service. The problem is that unions can be hard to get into.

# Secrets for Success

See the suggestions below and turn to the appendix for advice on résumés and interviews.

* Pay attention to directions. Remember, your creation is supposed to contribute to the production as a whole.
* It is your reputation that gets you more work. Let the people in charge of productions know they can count on you.

# Reality Check

Handicraftspersons get to work in an exciting, creative environment. However, the work can be irregular and sometimes stressful.

# Some Other Jobs to Think About

* Grip, stagehand, or set-up worker. Instead of making the scenery and props, why not move them around?
* Camera operator. Camera operators are an important part of shooting any film or TV.
* Computer animator. Computer animators are very important for adding special effects in post-production.

# *How You Can Move Up*

⭐ Become a designer. Many stage designers started on the bottom as handicraftspersons.

⭐ Learn a trade. Skilled workers such as carpenters and electricians are indispensable to theatrical productions—and a lot better paid!

⭐ Start your own company. If you become known for making model spaceships or stop-action dinosaurs, why not start a company specializing in that?

## Web Sites to Surf

**The Art Department.** An overview of what the art department is and what it does. From a UK site, but very relevant to American film industry as well. http://www.skillset.org/film/jobs/article_3645_1.asp

**IATSE.** The International Alliance of Theatrical Stage Employees, Moving Picture Technicians, Artists, and Allied Crafts—the union most craftspersons belong to. http://www.iatse-intl.org

Unlock your network

# Appendix A

Get your résumé ready

Ace your interview

# Putting Your Best Foot Forward

When 20-year-old Justin Schulman started job-hunting for a position as a fitness trainer—the first step toward managing a fitness facility—he didn't mess around. "I immediately opened the Yellow Pages and started calling every number listed under health and fitness, inquiring about available positions," he recalls. Schulman's energy and enterprise paid off: He wound up with interviews that led to several offers of part-time work.

Schulman's experience highlights an essential lesson for job seekers: There are plenty of opportunities out there, but jobs won't come to you—especially the career-oriented, well-paying ones that that you'll want to stick with over time. You've got to seek them out.

## Uncover Your Interests

Whether you're in high school or bringing home a full-time paycheck, the first step toward landing your ideal job is assessing your interests. You need to figure out what makes you tick. After all, there is a far greater chance that you'll enjoy and succeed in a career that taps into your passions, inclinations, and natural abilities. That's what happened with career-changer Scott Rolfe. He was already 26 when he realized he no longer wanted to work in the food industry. "I'm an avid outdoorsman," Rolfe says, "and I have an appreciation for natural resources that many people take for granted." Rolfe turned his passions into his ideal job as a forestry technician.

If you have a general idea of what your interests are, you're far ahead of the game. You may know that you're cut out for a health care career, for instance, or one in business. You can use a specific volume of Great Careers with a High School Diploma to discover what position to target. If you are unsure of your direction, check out the whole range of volumes to see the scope of jobs available.

You can also use interest inventories and skills-assessment programs to further pinpoint your ideal career. Your school or public librarian or guidance counselor should be able to help you locate such assessments. Web sites, such as America's Career InfoNet (http ://www.acinet.org) and Jobweb.com, also offer interest inventories.

You'll find suggestions for Web sites related to specific careers at the end of each chapter in any Great Careers with a High School Diploma volume.

## *Unlock* Your Network

The next stop toward landing the perfect job is networking. The word may make you cringe. But networking is simply introducing yourself and exchanging job-related and other information that may prove helpful to one or both of you. That's what Susan Tinker-Muller did. Quite a few years ago, she struck up a conversation with a fellow passenger on her commuter train. Little did she know that the natural interest she expressed in the woman's accounts payable department would lead to news about a job opening there. Tinker-Muller's networking landed her an entry-level position in accounts payable with MTV Networks. She is now the accounts payable administrator.

Tinker-Muller's experience illustrates why networking is so important. Fully 80 percent of openings are *never* advertised, and more than half of all employees land their jobs through networking, according to the U.S. Bureau of Labor Statistics. That's 8 out of 10 jobs that you'll miss if you don't get out there and talk with people. And don't think you can bypass face-to-face conversations by posting your résumé on job sites like Craigslist, Monster.com, and Hotjobs.com and then waiting for employers to contact you. That's so mid-1990s! Back then, tens of thousands, if not millions, of job seekers diligently posted their résumés on scores of sites. Then they sat back and waited . . . and waited . . . and waited. You get the idea. Big job sites have their place, of course, but relying solely on an Internet job search is about as effective throwing your résumé into a black hole.

Begin your networking efforts by making a list of people to talk to: teachers, classmates (and their parents), anyone you've worked with, neighbors, members of your church, synogogue, temple or mosque, and anyone you've interned or volunteered with. You can also expand your networking opportunities through the student sections of industry associations; attending or volunteering at industry events, association conferences, career fairs; and through job-shadowing. Keep in mind that only rarely will any of the people on your list be in a position to offer you a job. But whether they know it or not, they probably know someone who knows someone who is. That's why your networking goal is not to ask for a job but the name of someone to talk with. Even when you network with an employer, it's wise to say something like, "You may not have any positions available, but would you know someone I could talk with to find out more about what it's like to work in this field?"

Also, keep in mind that networking is a two-way street. For instance, you may be talking with someone who has a job opening that isn't appropriate for you. If you can refer someone else to the employer, either person may well be disposed to help you someday in the future.

# Dial-Up Help

Call your contacts directly, rather than e-mail them. (E-mails are too easy for busy people to ignore, even if they don't mean to.) Explain that you're a recent graduate; that Mr. Jones referred you; and that you're wondering if you could stop by for 10 or 15 minutes at your contact's convenience to find out a little more about how the industry works. If you leave this message as a voicemail, note that you'll call back in a few days to follow up. If you reach your contact directly, expect that they'll say they're too busy at the moment to see you. Ask, "Would you mind if I check back in a couple of weeks?" Then jot down a note in your date book or set up a reminder in your computer calendar and call back when it's time. (Repeat this above scenario as needed, until you get a meeting.)

Once you have arranged to talk with someone in person, prep yourself. Scour industry publications for insightful articles; having up-to-date knowledge about industry trends shows your networking contacts that you're dedicated and focused. Then pull together questions about specific employers and suggestions that will set you apart from the job-hunting pack in your field. The more specific your questions (for instance, about one type of certification versus another), the more likely your contact will see you as an "insider," worthy of passing along to a potential employer. At the end of any networking meeting, ask for the name of someone else who might be able to help you further target your search.

# Get a Lift

When you meet with a contact in person (as well as when you run into someone fleetingly), you need an "elevator speech." This is a summary of up to two minutes that introduces who you are, as well as your experience and goals. An elevator speech should be short enough to be delivered during an elevator ride with a potential employer from the ground level to a high floor. In it, it's helpful to show that 1) you know the business involved; 2) you know the company; 3) you're qualified (give your work and educational information); and 4) you're goal-oriented, dependable, and hardworking. You'll be surprised how much information you can include in two minutes. Practice this speech in front of a mirror until you have the key points down very well. It should sound natural though, and you should come across as friendly, confident, and assertive. Remember, good eye contact needs to be part of your presentation as well as your everyday approach when meeting prospective employers or leads.

## Get Your Résumé Ready

In addition to your elevator speech, another essential job-hunting tool is your résumé. Basically, a résumé is a little snapshot of you in words, reduced to one 8½ x 11-inch sheet of paper (or, at most, two sheets). You need a résumé whether you're in high school, college, or the workforce, and whether you've never held a job or have had many.

At the top of your résumé should be your heading. This is your name, address, phone numbers, and your e-mail address, which can be a sticking point. E-mail addresses such as sillygirl@yahoo.com or drinkingbuddy@hotmail.com won't score you any points. In fact they're a turn-off. So if you dreamed up your address after a night on the town, maybe it's time to upgrade. (And while we're on the subject, these days, potential employers often check Myspace pages, personal blogs, and Web sites. What's posted there has been known to cost candidates job offers.)

The first section of your résumé is a concise Job Objective: "Entry-level agribusiness sales representative seeking a position with a leading dairy cooperative." These days, with word-processing software, it's easy and smart to adapt your job objective to the position for which you're applying. An alternative way to start a résumé, which some recruiters prefer, is to rework the Job Objective into a Professional Summary. A Professional Summary doesn't mention the position you're seeking, but instead focuses on your job strengths: e.g., "Entry-level agribusiness sales rep; strengths include background in feed, fertilizer, and related markets and ability to contribute as a member of a sales team." Which is better? It's your call.

The body of a résumé typically starts with your Job Experience. This is a chronological list of the positions you've held (particularly the ones that will help you land the job you want). Remember: Never, never fudge anything. It is okay, however, to include volunteer positions and internships on the chronological list, as long as they're noted for what they are.

Next comes your Education section. Note: It's acceptable to flip the order of your Education and Job Experience sections if you're still in high school or don't have significant work experience. Summarize any courses you've taken in the job area you're targeting, any certifications you've achieved, relevant computer knowledge, special seminars, or other school-related experience that will distinguish you. Include your grade average if it's more than 3.0. Don't worry if you haven't finished your degree. Simply write that you're currently enrolled in your program (if you are).

In addition to these elements, other sections may include professional organizations you belong to and any work-related achievements, awards, or recognition you've received. Also, you can have a section for your interests, such as playing piano or soccer (and include any notable achievements regarding your interests, for instance, placed third in Midwest Regional Piano Competition). You should also note other special abilities, such as "Fluent in French," or "Designed own Web site." These sorts of activities will reflect well on you whether or not they are job-related.

You can either include your references or simply note, "References Upon Request." Be sure to ask your references permission to use their name, and alert them to the fact that they may be contacted, before you include them on your résumé. For more information on résumé writing, check out Web sites such as http://www.resume .monster.com.

## *Craft Your Cover Letter*

When you apply for a job either online or by mail, it's appropriate to include a cover letter. A cover letter lets you convey extra information about yourself than doesn't fit or isn't always appropriate in your résumé. For instance, in a cover letter, you can and should mention the name of anyone who referred you to the job. You can go into some detail about the reason you're a great match, given the job description. You can also address any questions that might be raised in the potential employer's mind (for instance, a gap in your résumé). Don't, however, ramble on. Your cover letter should stay focused on your goal: to offer a strong, positive impression of yourself and persuade the hiring manager that you're worth an interview. Your cover letter gives you a chance to stand out from the other applicants and sell yourself. In fact, 23 percent of hiring managers say a candidate's ability to relate his or her experience to the job at hand is a top hiring consideration, according to a Careerbuilder.com survey.

You can write a positive, yet concise cover letter in three paragraphs: An introduction containing the specifics of the job you're applying for; a summary of why you're a good fit for the position and what you can do for the company; and a closing with a request for an interview, your contact information, and thanks. Remember to vary the structure and tone of your cover letter. For instance, don't begin every sentence with "I."

## *Ace Your Interview*

Preparation is the key to acing any job interview. This starts with researching the company or organization you're interviewing with. Start with the firm, group, or agency's own Web site. Explore it thoroughly, read about their products and services, their history, and sales and marketing information. Check out their news releases, links that they provide, and read up on, or Google, members of the management team to get an idea of what they may be looking for in their employees.

Sites such as http://www.hoovers.com enable you to research companies across many industries. Trade publications in any industry (such as *Food Industry News*, *Hotel Business*, and *Hospitality Technology*) are also available at online or in hard copy at many college or public libraries. Don't forget to make a phone call to contacts you have in the organization to get a better idea of the company culture.

Preparation goes beyond research, however. It includes practicing answers to common interview questions:

✦ *Tell me about yourself.* Don't talk about your favorite bands or your personal history; give a brief summary of your background and interest in the particular job area.

✦ *Why do you want to work here?* Here's where your research into the company comes into play; talk about the firm's strengths and products or services.

* *Why should we hire you?* Now is your chance to sell yourself as a dependable, trustworthy, effective employee.
* *Why did you leave your last job?* Keep your answer short; never bad-mouth a previous employer. You can always say something simple, such as, "It wasn't a good fit, and I was ready for other opportunities."

Rehearse your answers, but don't try to memorize them. Responses that are natural and spontaneous come across better. Trying to memorize exactly what you want to say is likely to both trip you up and make you sound robotic.

As for the actual interview, to break the ice, offer a few pleasant remarks about the day, a photo in the interviewer's office, or something else similar. Then, once the interview gets going, listen closely and answer the questions you're asked, versus making any other point that you want to convey. If you're unsure whether your answer was adequate, simply ask, "Did that answer the question?" Show respect, good energy, and enthusiasm, and be upbeat. Employers are looking for workers who are enjoyable to be around, as well as good workers. Show that you have a positive attitude and can get along well with others by not bragging during the interview, overstating your experience, or giving the appearance of being too self-absorbed. Avoid one-word answers, but at the same time don't blather. If you're faced with a silence after giving your response, pause for a few seconds, and then ask, "Is there anything else you'd like me to add?" Never look at your watch and turn your cell phone off before an interview.

Near the interview's end, the interviewer is likely to ask you if you have any questions. Make sure that you have a few prepared, for instance:

* *"Tell me about the production process."*
* *"What's your biggest short-term challenge?"*
* *"How have recent business trends affected the company?"*
* *"Is there anything else that I can provide you with to help you make your decision?"*
* *"When will you make your hiring decision?"*

During a first interview, never ask questions like, "What's the pay?" "What are the benefits?" or "How much vacation time will I get?"

# *Find the Right Look*

Appropriate dress and grooming is also essential to interviewing success. For business jobs and many other occupations, it's appropriate to come to an interview in a nice (not stuffy) suit. However, different fields have various dress codes. In the music business, for instance, "business casual" reigns for many jobs. This is a slightly modified look, where slacks and a jacket are just fine for a man, and a nice skirt and blouse and jacket or sweater are acceptable for a woman. Dressing overly "cool" will usually backfire.

In general, tend to all the basics from shoes (no sneakers, sandals, or overly high heels) to outfits (no short skirts for women). Women should also avoid attention-getting necklines. Keep jewelry to a minimum. Tattoos and body jewelry are becoming more acceptable, but if you can take out piercings (other than a simple stud in your ear), you're better off. Similarly, unusual hairstyles or colors may bias an employer against you, rightly or wrongly. Make sure your hair is neat and acceptable (consider getting a haircut). Also go light on the makeup, self-tanning products, body scents, and other grooming agents. Don't wear a baseball cap or any other type of hat, and by all means, take off your sunglasses!

Beyond your physical appearance, you already know to be well bathed to minimize odor (leave your home early if you tend to sweat, so you can cool off in private), use a breath mint (especially if you smoke) make good eye contact, smile, speak clearly using proper English (or Spanish), use good posture (don't slouch), offer a firm handshake, and arrive within five minutes of your interview. (If you're unsure of where you're going, Mapquest or Google Map it and consider making a dry run to the site so you won't be late.) First impressions can make or break your interview.

# *Remember to Follow Up*

After your interview, send a thank-you note. This thoughtful gesture will separate you from most of the other candidates. It demonstrates your ability to follow through, and it catches your prospective employer's attention one more time. In a 2005 Careerbuilder.com survey, nearly 15 percent of 650 hiring managers said they wouldn't hire someone who failed to send a thank-you letter after the interview. Thirty-two percent say they would still consider the candidate, but would think less of him or her.

So do you hand write or e-mail the thank you letter? The fact is that format preferences vary. One in four hiring managers prefer to receive a thank-you note in e-mail form only; 19 percent want the e-mail, followed up with a hard copy; 21 percent want a typed hard-copy only, and 23 percent prefer just a handwritten note. (Try to check with an assistant on the format your potential employer prefers). Otherwise, sending an e-mail and a handwritten copy is a safe way to proceed.

# *Winning an Offer*

There are no sweeter words to a job hunter than, "We'd like to hire you." So naturally, when you hear them, you may be tempted to jump at the offer. *Don't.* Once an employer wants you, he or she will usually give you some time to make your decision and get any questions you may have answered. Now is the time to get specific about salary, benefits, and negotiate some of these points. If you haven't already done so, check out salary ranges for your position and area of the country on sites such as Payscale.com, Salary.com, and Salaryexpert.com (basic info is free; specific requests are not). Also find out what sort of benefits similar jobs offer. Then don't be afraid to negotiate in a diplomatic way. Asking for better terms is reasonable and expected. You may worry that asking the employer to bump up his or her offer may jeopardize your job, but handled intelligently, negotiating for yourself may in fact be a way to impress your future employer and get a better deal for yourself.

After you've done all the hard work that successful job-hunting requires, you may be tempted to put your initiative into autodrive. However, the efforts you made to land your job—from clear communication to enthusiasm—are necessary now to pave your way to continued success. As Danielle Little, a human-resources assistant, says, "You must be enthusiastic and take the initiative. There is an urgency to prove yourself and show that you are capable of performing any and all related tasks. If your manager notices that you have potential, you will be given additional responsibilities, which will help advance your career." So do your best work on the job, and build your credibility. Your payoff will be career advancement and increased earnings.

# Index